Venice Saved

Venice Saved

Simone Weil

Translated and Introduced by
Silvia Panizza and Philip Wilson,
University of East Anglia, UK

BLOOMSBURY ACADEMIC
LONDON · NEW YORK · OXFORD · NEW DELHI · SYDNEY

BLOOMSBURY ACADEMIC
Bloomsbury Publishing Plc
50 Bedford Square, London, WC1B 3DP, UK
1385 Broadway, New York, NY 10018, USA

BLOOMSBURY, BLOOMSBURY ACADEMIC and the Diana logo are
trademarks of Bloomsbury Publishing Plc

First published in Great Britain in 2019

Cover design by Maria Rajka
Cover image: *Italy, Venice, detail with Church of Redeemer and
St. George* by artist from Venetian School, 17th century / De Agostini
© Picture Library / A. Dagli Orti / Bridgeman Images

A catalogue record for this book is available from the British Library.

A catalog record for this book is available from the Library of Congress.

ISBN: PB: 978-1-3500-4390-9
ePDF: 978-1-3500-4391-6
eBook: 978-1-3500-4392-3

Typeset by Deanta Global Publishing Services, Chennai, India
Printed and bound in Great Britain

To find out more about our authors and books visit www.bloomsbury.com
and sign up for our newsletters.

Contents

Translators' Biographies

Silvia Panizza Lecturer in Ethics at the University of East Anglia, Medical School, having previously taught at Anglia Ruskin University and the University of Genoa. She works in moral philosophy, philosophy of religion and philosophy and/of literature, and has investigated the idea of attention in Simone Weil and Iris Murdoch. She has published on Weil and the possibility of secular mysticism, William Hazlitt, Lawrence Durrell and animal ethics. She has a chapter on Ludwig Wittgenstein in the *Routledge Handbook of Translation and Philosophy* (2019).

Philip Wilson teaches philosophy at the University of East Anglia. Publications include *The Luther Breviary* (translated with John Gledhill, 2007); *Literary Translation: Re-drawing the Boundaries* (edited with Jean Boase-Beier and Antoinette Fawcett, 2014); *The Bright Rose: German Verse 800-1280* (translated and edited, 2015); *Translation after Wittgenstein* (2015); *The Routledge Handbook of Translation and Philosophy* (edited with Piers Rawling, 2019); *Alexander Neville's Norwich Histories* (translated and edited with Ingrid Walton and Clive Wilkins-Jones, forthcoming). His research interests include the links between mysticism, esotericism and translation.

Preface

At the end of her life, in extremely difficult circumstances, the French philosopher Simone Weil (1909–43) worked on (but did not finish) her only play, *Venise Sauvée* (henceforth *Venice Saved*). It has been largely ignored and has never before been published in an English translation. Interest in Weil's work has increased massively since her death and continues to grow, so that publishing this play in English will enable readers to expand their view of this important writer.

Weil occupies a unique place in the philosophy of the twentieth century. She is not regarded as having changed the field like her contemporaries Martin Heidegger and Ludwig Wittgenstein. She published no major work in her lifetime and, unlike most major philosophers, never taught in a university. Yet her writings – philosophical, political and religious – continue to inspire many and she is the focus of a great deal of academic research. Her ongoing influence can be seen on authors who work *outside* professional philosophy, especially those involved in the creative arts: she is a protagonist in Anne Carson's poetic opera *Decreation* (2005); the film *An Encounter with Simone Weil* (2011) by Julia Haslett interprets Weil in the light of her contention that our damaged world needs attention; Kiaja Saariaho's musical oratorio *La Passion de Simone* (The Passion of Simone) (2013) blends Weil's life with the Stations of the Cross; a recent poem by Rebecca Tamás, 'Simone Weil', is a sensitive exploration of Weil's mystical form of life (2017: n.p.). That Weil herself produced creative writing – some poems and this play – is often overlooked by readers and provides an indirect way of approaching her philosophy, as well as being of interest in itself.

We have also translated the notes that Weil wrote about *Venice Saved* and her sketches for the unwritten scenes, and have written four introductory chapters on Weil's life and philosophy; how the play came to be written and what it has to say; Weil's view of tragedy; the issues raised by writing an English version of this drama. There are translators' notes on the play, suggestions for further reading and a bibliography of all works used in writing the introductory material.

Acknowledgements

We should like to thank our colleague Davide Rizza for suggesting the project to us in the first place and for being generous with his expert knowledge of Simone Weil. Our colleague Gareth Jones has offered constant support and philosophical advice and is due a great debt.

We are immensely grateful to Frankie Mace, our amazing editor at Bloomsbury, who accepted the project and offered constant encouragement and guidance along the way.

In addition, we have been fortunate to have had invaluable help with issues of elucidation and translation. Thank you to Coralie Bastiaens, Jean Boase-Beier, Jolanda Caprioglio, Tomeu Estelrich, Marc Fielder, Tony Gash, Alice Leal, Giulio Panizza, A. Rebecca Rozelle-Stone, Max Schleicher, Gabriël Maes, Stephen Spencer, Helen Tierney and Ingrid Walton. We should also like to thank Bloomsbury's two anonymous reviewers for their excellent advice. Any errors or omissions are of course our own.

Our discussions of the life of Simone Weil draw on the chronology and the autobiographical writings and letters in Florence de Lussy's 1999 edition of Weil's works (Weil 1999); Richard Rees's translation of *Seventy Letters* (Weil 1965); biographical work by Gabriella Fiori (1989), Simone Pétrement (1976) and Stephen Plant (2007).

Silvia Panizza
Philip Wilson

List of Abbreviations

In the introductory material and the translators' notes, we reference Weil's work by abbreviated title and page and thus (GG 50) is a reference to *Gravity and Grace* page 50. Full details of books used are in the bibliography. Weil's works are abbreviated as follows:

APP   *On the Abolition of All Political Parties* (2014)

GG   *Gravity and Grace* (2003)

IC   *Intimations of Christianity among the Ancient Greeks* (1957)

IP   'The Iliad, or The Poem of Force' (2005)

LP   *Letter to a Priest* (2002a)

LPW   *Late Philosophical Writings* (2015)

NB   *The Notebooks of Simone Weil* (1951)

NR   *The Need for Roots* (2002)

O   *Œuvres* (1999)

OL   *Oppression and Liberty* (2001)

PVS   *Poèmes suivis de Venise sauvée, Lettre de Paul Valéry* (1968)

SL   *Seventy Letters* (1965)

WG   *Waiting for God* (1978)

Simone Weil: An Inhabited Philosophy

Sarah Bakewell calls Weil's life a 'profound and challenging application of Iris Murdoch's notion that a philosophy can be "inhabited"' (2016: 199). In this introductory chapter, we explore aspects of this inhabited philosophy in order to read Simone Weil's *Venice Saved* in its history. Weil was adamant that it was her thought that mattered. She wrote to Joseph-Marie Perrin that she did not want people to take an interest in her life but to look at her ideas and decide whether they were true or not (Pétrement 1976: vii). However, even if Simone Pétrement is right to argue that we can never explain whether a thinker's work is *true* by looking at his or her life (Pétrement 1976: vii), knowledge of historical context places us in a better position to understand her work. Writing on George Herbert, for example, John Drury asserts that the 'circumstances of a poet's life and times are the soil in which the work is rooted – not just the outward and material circumstances but also, and still more, the inward patterns of thought and feeling prevailing in the poet's world' (2014: xvi). We should read philosophers *in* history. No matter how sublime the metaphysics of Martin Heidegger is, for example, no matter how astute his observations on the natural world or on translation are, his active involvement with Nazism makes some people hesitate about what he wrote. Many readers, on the other hand, find an appeal in Ludwig Wittgenstein that 'might be said to be based on the way philosophical truth comes together with a certain conception of existential meaning, indeed a certain way of life' (Critchley 2001: 11; cf. Hadot 1995). Something similar is true of Weil, a woman whose commitment to truth took her into school teaching, political activism, factory work, the Spanish Civil War and intellectual labour for the Free French government in exile in London. For her, philosophy was not a matter of solving metaphysical problems in academic papers, but a lived reality.

Weil began to write *Venice Saved* in 1940, the year in which France fell to German forces. She based it on a historical fiction published in 1674 by the Abbé de Saint-Réal (César Vichard), which is also the source for Thomas Otway's highly successful 1682 tragedy *Venice Preserv'd* (1976). Weil's play is incomplete, though she wrote comments about it and sketched out prose ideas for the unwritten scenes. As Richard Rees comments, 'The completed parts of the text, read in conjunction with the author's numerous notes and memoranda, which are published as a preface, compose a whole which can be read and understood almost as if it were a finished work' (1958: 191). The project was important to Weil. In a letter of 1937 she had asked why she could not have the 'n existences' she needed, in order to devote one of them to the theatre (SL 91). She frequently mentioned the play to friends, showed them work in progress, made various drafts and at the end of her life asked for her notes together with a copy of the play to be sent to her in London. Only her death in 1943 prevented her from completing it.

No claim is being made here that *Venice Saved* is a work of literary genius. Its main interest lies in the fact that an important and much researched *philosophical* genius should have written a tragedy. What can this tell us about Weil? And what themes in the tragedy are of philosophical value? The play itself, however, is by no means without merits, as shown by Serena Nono's recent film (2013). We believe that it is time to publish an English translation, given the continued popular and scholarly interest in Weil, because this is a text that presents both the political and metaphysical views that Weil had been working out towards the end of her life (see Fiori 1989: 187).

Venice Saved is a play, a dramatic poem, a work of literature. It presents a Spanish conspiracy in 1618 to overthrow Venice and subjugate its people. The conspiracy fails because Jaffier, one of the conspirators' leaders, is affected by pity for the beauty of Venice and betrays the plans to the Council of Ten, on the assurance that his friends' lives will be spared. The city is saved but the promise to Jaffier is not honoured. A broken man, he finally joins what is left of the conspiracy in order to die fighting. The play thus can be read as a literary study of the nature of force, affliction, attention and friendship, informed by philosophical reflection.

The French literary canon contains many works by philosophers. Simone de Beauvoir, Albert Camus, Denis Diderot, Jean-Paul Sartre, Jean-Jacques Rousseau and Voltaire have all produced novels and plays that are read and studied today. The literary is in any case a blurred concept. A great deal of philosophical writing has literary merit, and a great deal of literary writing offers profound philosophical insights. Plato's philosophical dialogue *The Symposium* involves a carefully constructed story and includes as many literary features as any novel; Tolstoy's historical novel *War and Peace* raises profound philosophical issues about history and the human condition. Narrative is, after all, an important aspect of being human; we respond to ideas when they are found in stories, whether about a dinner party in Athens, Napoleon's attack on Russia or a failed conspiracy in Venice. Jean Boase-Beier argues that 'poems are not separate from either ways of thinking or ways of feeling: they are those ways of thinking and feeling poeticized' (2015: 6). *Venice Saved* thus both illustrates the thought of Weil and shows it in a different light. Just as readers and scholars turn to the novels and plays of Sartre in order to investigate his philosophy, so *Venice Saved* can serve as a way in to Weil's thought, especially because we have privileged access to the process of writing because of her remarks and sketches for the unwritten scenes.

Weil is also a significant philosophical figure because she is a woman in a male-dominated field. In the early twenty-first century, when the underrepresentation of women in both canonical and contemporary philosophy is under critical investigation (see Hutchison and Jenkins 2013), it is clearly important to make work by women philosophers available to as many readers as possible. She has even been viewed as a feminist icon (Plant 2007: xiv), and Gabriella Fiori argues that it is impossible to separate the fact that she was a genius from the fact that she was a woman (1989: 309 ff.). There are, however, problems with seeing her as an icon. She never engaged with the issues that dominate the feminist work of de Beauvoir, for example, and in Weil's writings there is a general lack of intellectual interest on the situation of women. Again, her Platonism means that there she is more interested in the world of the spirit than in embodiment, which places her in opposition to many feminist thinkers, including Christian feminist thinkers (cf. Clack 2015). The main female character in *Venise Sauvée*, Violetta, is flat and uninteresting, functioning very obviously as a cipher for the beauty of Venice. By contrast, the courtesan is portrayed in greater depth. We hear her tell of why she has turned to prostitution and see her lively interactions with the mercenaries. (Weil was herself interested in the plight of prostitutes. In 1937, she visited a brothel disguised as a young man in order to see what went on but was quickly discovered and chased out.)

To study Weil's work is to encounter a philosopher in the French tradition. She matches the five characteristics of French thought sketched by Sudhir Hazareesingh (2015: 17): her work is historical, looking to the past for legitimation; it is fixated with the nation and the collective self; it shows an extraordinary intensity with respect to ideas, which not only matter but are worth dying for; it shows a need to communicate to a wider public; there is a constant interplay between order and the imagination. We can discern in particular an engagement with the imagination in *Venice Saved*, especially if we pay attention to the paratextual material.

At the Lycée Henri VI in Paris, which she entered aged sixteen, Weil showed promise in philosophy and was taught by the celebrated philosopher Émile Chartier (known as Alain), who exercised a profound influence on her thinking. Weil adopted his method of philosophy, which was based on the close reading of primary texts. (What frequently strikes the reader of Weil is the breadth of both her writing and reading. She produced a large corpus in a short life, drawing extensively on classical and modern philosophy, world literature and religious writings.) Alain also introduced her to Plato, who would be the major philosophical influence on her thought, and impressed on her the need to write with clarity. She progressed to the elite École Normale Supérieure, graduating in 1931 with a degree in philosophy. Her thesis was on science and perception in Descartes.

Her Platonism and stress on the world of the spirit can be linked to her ascetic lifestyle. She was always reluctant to seek comfort in a world where others were in pain, and would precipitate her own death by refusing to eat properly in solidarity with the people of occupied France, which meant that *Venice Saved* remained unfinished. She lived through the First World War, in which her father served as an army surgeon, and was aware of the suffering caused by the conflict, giving up sugar in solidarity with the troops. From 1930 she suffered from severe headaches that would frequently disable her, and that showed her the meaning of 'affliction', a major theme in her later thought and in *Venice Saved*, where Jaffier becomes an 'afflicted man' after he has betrayed the plot. Her asceticism was not, however, without human traits: she enjoyed activities such as skiing and swimming, loved to travel, showed great kindness to friends – an important issue in the play – and (as befits a French philosopher of that era) was a heavy smoker. Weil was also profoundly attached to literature, music and art, and was a fan of Charlie Chaplin's *Modern Times*. This human side can be discerned in *Venice Saved*, which is based on wide reading and which portrays the beauty of a city, written by somebody with a keen awareness of what the world can offer, as well as of the affliction that arises when force is resisted. Violetta's lyrical evocation of Venice – the 'city of stone and water' – that ends the play is an example of this awareness.

For Weil, philosophy could never be purely academic but demanded political involvement. When she worked between 1931 and 1934 in schools as a teacher of philosophy and literature, she continued her student political activism, leading the unemployed in their struggles against injustice in Le Puy, for example. Her political views were always of the left, but she was never a member of the Communist Party, probably due to her distrust of organizations. She even argued that political parties should be abolished (see APP). In 1932, she visited Germany to investigate Nazism and foresaw what the rise to power of Hitler would mean, fearing that the left was too disunited to combat it. She published some of her political reflections (for small readerships) at this time and frequently became involved in controversy because she had the courage to go against party lines. Fiori calls her a political 'heretic' (1989: 84 ff.). She was aware of the injustices of Stalin's Russia and wrote against them with insight, arguing that the Russian Revolution had failed the proletariat and had instituted the tyranny of bureaucracy. For her, problems of force were perennial, which meant that all revolutionary theories would fail to produce a better world, just as the imposition of force on Venice will lead to murder and rape and the destruction of beauty, even though the conspirators speak at length of the Christian Europe under Spanish hegemony that they claim as their guiding vision.

Weil met and argued with Leon Trotsky, who called her a reactionary with doubts about everything and asked if she had joined the Salvation Army. Trotsky was wrong. Weil was both a woman of ideas and a woman of action. She was never content merely to theorize about political questions but felt the need to get involved in events. She was, revealingly, an admirer of the intellectual soldier T. E. Lawrence, author of *The Seven Pillars of Wisdom*, whom she called an 'authentic hero' (SL 93). She devised a plan for women (including herself) to serve on the front line as nurses (SL 145–53), and when working for the Free French in London she demanded to be sent to occupied France as a Resistance operative. This need to match conviction with action led her to undertake work in factories in 1934–5 and then to participate in the Spanish Civil War in 1936. She is a world away from the sort of intellectual who never encounters the workers or the victims for whom she claims to speak. Factory work broke her health as she spent long hours on monotonous and dehumanizing machine work, trying when possible to educate her fellow operators and writing up her thoughts. For her it was necessary to have what Nassim Nicholas Taleb calls 'skin in the game'; her year in factories meant that 'the working class could be something other than an abstract construct for her' (Taleb 2018: 184). The need to have skin in the game also meant that the pacifist Weil felt that she had to take up arms with the Republicans against Franco's fascist forces in Spain. Similarly, Jaffier must act when he realizes what will happen to the beauty of Venice if the conspiracy succeeds, even though his action means betraying both his ambition and his friends, including his very best friend, his beloved Pierre, thus bringing about his own moral and physical destruction. Weil saw little action in Spain because she stepped into a pot of boiling fat and had to be invalided home, but the Spanish experience gave her first-hand acquaintance with war and its horrors, which is an important theme in her play. No matter how grandiose the conspirators' plans for forming a new colony are, the conquest of Venice would lead to terrible human suffering. Weil had a particular horror of sexual violence and it is significant how she foregrounds this aspect of warfare at key points of the tragedy, as the mercenaries describe in horrible detail what they will do to the women of Venice once they have taken power. She wrote in 1938 to the Catholic right-wing novelist Georges Bernanos, describing the atrocities she had heard of in the Spanish Civil War, such as the young nationalist 'hero' who refused to renounce his fascism and was summarily executed.

She argued that the issue here is the attitude taken towards 'murder' (SL 105–9). Jaffier must similarly acknowledge that it is murder that awaits Venice, not the ruthlessness that is necessary to ensure a glorious political takeover. He must therefore betray his principles in the face of reality. Weil had similarly renounced pacifism totally by 1939 in recognition of the threat posed by Hitler, and we will discuss in Chapter 2 how the conspiracy against Venice as depicted by Weil can be read against the military expansion of the Third Reich, which had caused her to flee her homeland, aware of the invaders' attitude to Jews.

Weil was born to a non-religious Jewish family and her outlook throughout her formative years was secular. Today, however, she is studied and read by many people for the Christian writings that dominate her later output. A major change in Weil's world view had taken place in the 1930s, brought about by three encounters with Catholicism. In 1935, she visited a Portuguese fishing village where she was profoundly moved by a Catholic festival, becoming convinced that Christianity was the religion of slaves, a category with which she had come to identify after her work in industry. Then in 1937 she visited Assisi, where Saint Francis had carried out his mission, and was deeply impressed by the art and the Franciscan spirit, feeling herself forced to go down to her knees for the first time in her life. In 1938, she attended the Holy Week and Easter services at the Benedictine Abbey of Solesmes, where the liturgy gave her a sense of mystical closeness to the afflicted Christ. She also came across George Herbert's poem 'Love' – an indication of the importance of literature for her as a form of telling the truth – in which the unworthy soul is visited and reassured by a loving God. Weil learned by heart what she called the most beautiful poem in the world and would later adopt prayer as a practice, saying the Lord's Prayer in Greek by heart and with absolute attention. Her later work stresses such need for attention in all things if we are to escape the gravity of our condition and have access to the transcendent realm. By looking attentively at a situation, we should know what to do, no matter how much it costs.

Her thought accordingly underwent a theological turn as she strove to reconcile her new metaphysics of transcendence with Catholic teaching (see *Waiting for God* (1978) and *Letter to a Priest* (2002b)). For her, the Church was Catholic by right but not in fact, and was guilty of totalitarianism. Too much truth – Greek philosophy, Indian mysticism and so on – lay outside it for her ever to be able to ask for baptism, although she spoke to and corresponded with a number of priests about receiving the sacrament. Fiori argues, 'Her nonbaptism was her testimony to the Christian faith' (1989: 317). Weil is difficult to categorize as a religious thinker because of the wide range of her interests. She can, however, be linked to Neo-Platonic and Gnostic tendencies in Western thought because of her insistence that Christianity has its true origins in Greek philosophy and literature, rather than in the Old Testament or the Roman Empire, to both of which she expressed antipathy, including in the notes to *Venice Saved*. Stephen Plant draws parallels between her thought and Catharism, a broadly Gnostic faith that flourished in mediaeval Languedoc before being brutally suppressed by the Catholic Church and the Kingdom of France, and in which Weil was interested (2007: 87ff.). He also argues that in her religious philosophy Weil was the 'player in a truth-game in which she was also the umpire' (2007: 98). Whether this should worry us depends upon our view of religion. If we see religion consisting in revealed truth, then her position is problematic. If we see religion as a human construct, or if we believe that philosophy can lead us to the truth, then we do not need to reject her opinions. In 1940, she wrote an important essay on Homer's *Iliad* (2005), which blends Christian and Greek worldviews. By Catholic standards it is heretical. But on its own terms, it creates a new and original form of the mystical.

Weil's work was originally preserved from oblivion by Christian scholars and readers. It is now possible to see broader metaphysical and political concerns in her writing, and certainly *Venice Saved* is no crude apologia for a religious world view, even if a Christian interpretation can be brought to the play: despite the Catholic background of Venice, overtly religious tropes are absent. Her hostility to the Old Testament and to Judaism in general and her silence about the persecution of the Jews by the Third Reich and its Vichy allies is, however, problematic in our post-Holocaust context where anti-Semitism continues to flourish. She refused, for example, to accept those parts of the Old Testament that in her opinion showed a violent God. When, in her notes for Act Two of *Venice Saved*, she writes of evoking the Old Testament in the context of the planned sack of Venice, this is not a positive move but an indication of a deity who takes pleasure in the destruction and humiliation of enemies. Sylvie Weil recounts denying being related to her aunt Simone when she heard her described as an anti-Semite who had converted to Catholicism (2009: 15–16); both statements are contestable, but a general problem is indicated.

Her three encounters with Catholicism – in Portugal, Assisi and Solesmes – show the importance of place to her when conceptualizing the sacred, and her attitude to Venice can also be seen in this light. In 1938, she visited Venice and took tours of the city and the region. As Fiori puts it, in *Venice Saved* the city will 'reemerge, marvellous and enchanting, as the symbolic city of nourishment for a human society' (1989: 163). As a Platonist, beauty was for Weil one of the main ways in which we can move towards the transcendent. The development of the mystical tendency in her thought did not mean, however, that she turned her back on politics. Her great political book *The Need for Roots* (2002a), written at the same time as *Venice Saved* when she was involved in the Free French 'think tank' in London, is in many aspects the product of her philosophical mysticism, and political themes obsessed her throughout her entire life, such as the plight of workers or the problems caused by colonialism.

We can therefore agree with Fiori on the relationship between Weil the afflicted author and Jaffier the afflicted saviour of Venice:

> Jaffier, who symbolizes the opposition of the principle of weakness to the dictation of force which has always dominated history, prefigures with his madness a project that Simone was bringing to maturity, of equal opposition. She is Jaffier. (1989: 188)

Both of them inhabit a philosophy.

But what of Weil today? Given her early death and the troubled circumstances of her life, her work has had to a large extent to be reconstructed. She never prepared a book for publication. Some of her most popular works, such as *Gravity and Grace* and *Letter to a Priest*, are edited anthologies, and her writings have only become available gradually. *La Pesanteur et la Grâce* (*Gravity and Grace*) was the first book by Weil to be published after her death (in 1947), a themed selection from her notebooks by Gustave Thibon, the Catholic farmer and theologian for whom she had worked after her flight from Paris to unoccupied France. It is a selection that makes her appear more Catholic than is the case, which is indicative of the sort of problems that arise with posthumously published work. Since then, most of her writings have appeared in French and most of these have been translated into English. The first volume of her *Œuvres Complètes* (*Complete Works*), edited by Florence de Lussy, was published in 1988 – in all there will be fifteen volumes – and a useful single-volume compendium *Œuvres* (*Works*) came out in 1999. In addition, there has been a massive amount of secondary literature published, in English as well as in French. Societies for the study of her thought exist in France and the United States. There is a quarterly French periodical devoted to her, the *Cahiers Simone Weil* (*Notebooks of Simone Weil*). Weil has found an audience since her death that was denied to her in life. Her work has appealed to philosophers – Iris Murdoch being an important example – as well as to those seeking spiritual and political guidance in confused times. In 1978, Simone Pétrement's *La Vie de Simone Weil* (*The Life of Simone Weil*) was published, a fine biography by a scholar of Gnosticism who had been Weil's friend since meeting her at the Lycée Henri VI. It has been translated into English and has been followed by a number of other biographical works, as well as aesthetic responses, such as those described in the Preface.

In such a situation, the existence of a play, even in unfinished form, becomes more significant, because it offers new readerly ways of contributing to a mosaic, of constructing a philosophy and a philosopher (cf. Plant 2007: 21–4). Weil remains a liminal figure, an outsider and yet also, as Susan Sontag puts it, 'the person who is excruciatingly identical with her ideas, the person who is rightly regarded as one of the most uncompromising and troubling witnesses to the modern travail of the spirit' (1963). Her tragedy *Venice Saved* is part of that witnessing.

The Genesis and Purport of *Venice Saved*

Simone Weil saw universal forces and principles lying under the surface of history, manifesting themselves in the political events of the ancient world just as in the events that took place during her life. The visible unfolding of facts was a sign of something deeper and more general. The same idea informs her historical tragedy and is part of its powerful resonance and significance. As Weil's biographer Gabriella Fiori writes, '*Venice Saved* presents in a poetic microcosm the ideas and the intuitions which Simone had been expressing in her political essays' (Fiori 1989: 187). It is possible for us to read *Venice Saved* as a reflection of the political turmoil that Weil was living through during the Second World War, or as a reflection of the history of colonial empires, from Rome to Napoleon. But to read different political and historical incidents into this play is possible only because of what, according to Weil, underlies all of these different events, namely, the principles of force – a natural tendency of mankind towards force through collectivity and the denial of key needs of the human soul that are caused by force in a process of uprooting. These ideas and the ways in which, according to Weil, they shape history are represented in distilled form in her Venetian play.

Weil's Sources

The historically disputed events of 1618 inspired other fictional accounts before Weil's, of which the most notable are *La conjuration des Espagnols contre la république de Venise* (1674) (*The Conspiracy of the Spanish Against the Republic of Venice*) by the Abbé de Saint-Réal (César Vichard); *Venice Preserv'd* (1682) by Thomas Otway and *Das gerettete Venedig* (*The Saved Venice*) (1905) by Hugo von Hofmannsthal. Both Weil and Otway took Saint-Réal as their source, while von Hofmannsthal followed Otway's model. Weil was also aware of Otway's version and took the title from him.

A look at the differences between Weil's play and her sources can illuminate the distinctive traits of her work. In Saint-Réal's prose account, the plot is instigated by Don Pedro, Duke of Osuna, who wants to destroy Venice and rule over it, and the Marquis de Bedmar, Spanish ambassador to Venice. The Jaffier figure, here called Balthasar Juven, is a Frenchman who betrays the conspiracy to the Doge. Osuna and Bedmar are spared, too powerful to be touched, and return to where they came from. Up to 3,000 men are executed. Saint-Réal's work has the tones of melodrama and is set up as a tragedy, with the aim of showing human behaviour in extreme circumstances. One fact is remarkably different from Weil's play: Juven betrays the conspiracy out of cowardice; after hearing the tortures that may follow, he gives in and reveals the plot. In his introduction, Andrée Mansau also notes that Saint-Réal depicts an 'original universe in which the heroes are victims of courtesans, of the Inquisition, of power and of the vanity of human passions' (Mansau 1977: 4; our translation). Nothing could be further from Weil's universe.

Thomas Otway's version, a tragic melodrama, was livelier and more successful, although with a fairly convoluted plot. In Otway, women (and the passion and lust they apparently arouse) are central to the development of the plot. Pierre enters the conspiracy mainly because of anger towards Antonio, the Venetian senator who slept with his mistress, the courtesan Aquilina, while he was away. Jaffeir (*sic*) is married to Belvidera ('Violetta' in Weil), the daughter of another Venetian senator, Priuli, who does not approve of the marriage. Interestingly, while Weil's female characters are flat, Otway gives them great complexity and also takes the opportunity to present women's struggles, Belvidera being torn between father and husband, unable to act as an independent agent.

As we are beginning to see, the differences with Weil's play are manifold, but two stand out: in Otway, the Venetian senate is corrupt, and we feel immediate sympathy for those who dislike the Venetians. Second, and more importantly, in Otway's play the motives for revealing the conspiracy are Jaffeir's love for his wife, who persuades him not to commit such vile deeds as he had planned, and revenge on Renault who tried to rape her. Finally, Pierre learns of Jaffeir's betrayal and Jaffeir is given the opportunity to see Pierre before his execution and obtain his forgiveness. In that scene, Jaffeir kills Pierre in order to preserve his honour and prevent his execution at the hands of the Venetians, then he kills himself in an act of atonement.

Despite the similarity in the subject matter, Otway and Weil wrote two completely different plays. Otway's play is overtly political (intended as an attack on the Whig party, and the plot as a representation of the Gunpowder Plot of 1605), and entirely lacks Weil's metaphysical dimension. The sexual relationships and human weaknesses presented by Otway were of no interest to Weil. The resolution and atonement present in Otway would have been impossible for Weil, who intended to present Jaffier as a figure of affliction, where no mitigation or resolution is possible.

The motive for revealing the conspiracy, both in Saint-Réal and in Otway, is probably the most significant point of divergence from Weil. According to Weil's biographer Simone Pétrement, Weil maintained that

Otway and others had not understood the nobility of the motive which, according to Saint-Réal, led Jaffier to denounce the plot: pity for the city. Such a rare sentiment must have seemed impossible to them, to the extent that they invented other motives. But it was this very motive that made the beauty of this story, and it seemed to her that she was the first to realise this. (1976: 365)

The idea that Jaffier could sacrifice so much out of pity for a city could not have occurred to Saint-Réal or Otway. It is an idea that is deeply rooted in Weil's metaphysics, and will be examined at some length in Chapter 3. The same metaphysical intent underlies Weil's reading of the (partially) historical events, which also take on a very different significance in the context of her play and of her thought.

History in Venice Saved

The historical truth of the story on which these artistic works are based is uncertain. In her notes to the play, Weil acknowledges this, but also notes that it is 'absolutely certain that the Council of Ten had several hundred men executed and that Bedmar had to leave Venice'. Historian John Julius Norwich confirms some suspected murders, at the exact same time: two bodies appeared on 18 May 1618, just after the Festival of the Wedding of the Sea and just before the arrival of a newly elected Doge (Norwich 2003: 522).

The Marquis of Bedmar, Spanish ambassador in Venice, did have to leave the city after a period of unrest and there is evidence that groups of adventurers and mercenaries were hoping to sack the city, but it is not clear to what extent and what sort of involvement Bedmar had in it (Preto 1996: 313). The idea of an international plot to conquer Venice first appeared in the work of the anti-Spanish Venetian Paolo Sarpi: it is on this source that Saint-Réal drew for his work (Hillgarth 2000: 523). From the name of the most famous person suspected of being involved, the alleged events became known as 'the Bedmar conspiracy'. Interestingly, Sarpi's account, written as the official version of the Venetian Republic, was not published at the time, perhaps to avoid panic spreading among Venetians, or not to corrupt the public image of Venice as a place of indestructible peace and stability (Sarpi 1834).

The myth of Venice as paragon of constitutional order and political wisdom must have influenced Weil when thinking about the play. Since the fourteenth century, the idea of Venice as the perfect society, a mix of democracy, monarchy and aristocracy, started to spread. Giorgio da Trebisonda claimed that Venice was an incarnation of Plato's *Laws* (Gaeta 1970). This myth helps to sustain the horror at the possible destruction of Venice in the play, and further stresses the contrast between the Venetians and their just political organization, and the Spanish, whose imperialistic aspirations mark them as symbol of injustice and disharmony. This contrast is, as we shall see, an important key to Weil's thought.

The myth found fertile ground in Weil's personal affinity with Italy as a whole, a country for which she could not help feeling, on her return from a journey there, a sense of 'Heimweh' or nostalgia for one's native country (Fiori 1989: 164). In the two journeys to Italy in 1937, Weil was delighted by the art, the people, the simplicity, the food, the joie de vivre. Italy seemed like an enchanted place to Weil and she was struck by the beauty to be found there, the very beauty which saves the city of Venice in her play, and which has an important role in her religious metaphysics (as we shall see in Chapter 3).

However, it would be wrong to conclude that Weil has a naïve and univocal image of Venice in mind. As the myth of Venice as paragon of political order started to be opposed (for instance, by Benedetto da Dei in the fifteenth century and by Jean Bodin in the sixteenth century), Weil can see that ruthlessness and force are not alien to the Venetian ruling class in the seventeenth century, as the characters of her play testify. The speech given by the Secretary of the Council of Ten in Act Three, on the necessity to suppress any opposition and not to give way to pity, is intended to match, as Weil notes, 'almost word for word Renaud's words about how Venice is to be treated in Act Two Scene Six'. Weil is under no illusion that a perfect government is to be found and that lower drives and the rule of force are absent even from an apparently peaceful state.

Weil's social philosophy, it is clear, is too refined to ignore the complexities of the political situation she is portraying. This does not mean, however, that the differences between Spain and Venice, as represented in the play, do not run deep. By opposing the imperial power of Spain to the city state of Venice, Weil is trying to set up a fundamental contrast that runs deeper than any actual political force: the contrast between the 'social' and the 'city'.

The 'Social' as the Great Beast

Weil makes this contrast very clear in her notes to the play. Spain represents 'the idea of empire', which is 'social without roots, social without city ... Spain: the conspiracy is something social for the conspirators. Venice is a city. "City" does not evoke the social'.

We can make sense of this opposition by appealing to Weil's idea of the 'social' and her more general distaste for groups of different sorts. Weil thought that individuals, by coming together as a group, give way to collective passions which, on the one hand, take them further and further from the truth, and on the other, exercise pressure on individual minds to the detriment of independent thought. In the essay 'On the Abolition of All Political Parties' (2014), written in 1943 at the very end of her life, Weil argues that political parties have such an effect, being by their nature devoted to their own preservation and growth by generating collective passions and by exercising collective pressure on the individuals. A party, for Weil, cannot exist outside of this mechanism. The same limitless growth, the same devouring impetus, resolved in the exercise of 'force' and led by passion and not intellect (and thus, Weil thought, not truth-seeking) is precisely what characterizes the 'social'. Expansionist powers, such as Spain in the play, or Germany at the time Weil was writing, follow these laws necessarily. As J. P. Little notes, in Weil's play it is not only the Spanish Empire that absorbs the individual and removes responsibility from her but the conspiracy itself. Renaud and Jaffier present their role in the plot as something above the ordinary, including above ordinary morality. What matters is that they will 'make history' and be remembered. In Act Two Scene Two, Renaud encourages Jaffier with these words:

> You are going to make history. You will destroy a power that is tyrannical, full of intrigue, hated by its own citizens and which opposes the unity of Europe. Thanks to you, the whole of Europe will be united under the Habsburg dynasty, and the ships of this united Europe will cross the seas to conquer the entire globe.

This is just what, as Weil writes (in NR), Hitler wanted above all: to be rewarded not by the goodness of deeds, but by fame (Little 1979: 300–1). And an expansionist kind of fame too.

Weil traces this idea of 'the social' back to Plato's Great Beast (*Republic*, Book VI): 'Plato compared society to a huge beast which men are forced to serve and which they are weak enough to worship' (OL 155). In the passages referred to, those who study the great beast of society become dependent on it, to the extent that they start losing a true sense of good and evil and believe them to be just what the beast likes and does not like. The observer of society 'describes things as good or bad according to its [the beast's] likes and dislikes, and can't justify his usage of the term any further' (*Republic* 493c).

The power of the beast, Weil warns, is immense. She comments that 'the Great Beast is the only object of idolatry, the only *ersatz* of God, the only imitation of something which is infinitely far from me and which is I myself' (GG 164). In the human search for ends,

Weil continues, it is impossible to take either oneself or another person as ends, as we know of our own limitations and therefore of others' limitations too: 'Only one thing can be taken as an end, for in relation to the human person it possesses a kind of transcendence: this is the collective' (GG 164). The collective is me but also beyond me: in this way, it acquires a validity that is self-awarded but seems objective: 'The power of the social element. Agreement between several men brings with it a feeling of reality. It brings with it also a sense of duty. Divergence, where this agreement is concerned, appears as a sin' (GG 167). All of this is extremely dangerous. As we have seen, the collective is neither truth-seeking nor morally good. Venerating society, coming to believe that what society wants is right and that disagreement with it is sinful, captures one in a web out of which it may be impossible to break free.

Thus the conspirators in *Venice Saved* never question their deeds. Their moral feelings, even their friendships, become nothing in the face of the group's planned goal. They mutually reinforce their motivation to act and seem caught in a system that leaves them little room for reflection. Jaffier's hesitation is immediately spotted, and the reaction is both disbelief (Pierre) and repression (Renaud). The mercenaries only desire to destroy Venice, rape the women and sack the houses. Their hunger, like the hunger of the beast, is palpable.

In the same way, the Spanish Empire, juxtaposed with the Venetian city state, only desires to incorporate it – or swallow it. The social beast just wants to exist and to preserve its existence. But that implies, at the same time, that it cannot allow anything else to exist: it is wholly devoted to its own preservation and all of its attention is directed to itself, to the exclusion of any different form of life outside of itself. For this reason it is 'always totalitarian' (NB 620). It is not difficult here to see the resonance of this claim, which in the play applies to Spain and the conspirators, extend into the history of the twentieth century and the events that Weil was living through.

Venice, the city, is by contrast in Weil's mind a place of culture, where intellect dominates passions, and where individuals are not subjected to the power of the beast. As Richard Rees writes, the city 'is a human environment in which men can be rooted and can find nourishment for their souls' (Rees 1958: 194).

Roots and Rootlessness

The above comment leads us to another striking and important aspect of the contrast between Venice and Spain: the latter – the social – is without roots, while the former is 'rooted'. The idea of rootlessness seems to be one of the main factors in Venice's superiority and one of the main reasons for the deep hatred that the Spanish mercenaries feel for the Venetians. The mercenaries, and the conspirators in general, lack roots; the Venetians have roots. For the uprooted, relief comes by destroying those who are not plagued by the same absence: Renaud savours in anticipation the moment, after the capture, when in Venice 'the children ... will be born without roots' (Act Two Scene Six).

Weil writes the following in her notes: 'it must be apparent that this is a conspiracy of exiles, of uprooted men' who 'all hate the Venetians for having a home – apart from Jaffier. (Yes, even Pierre.)' Renaud, Jaffier and Pierre are exiles, the first from France and the other two from Provence. This fact is significant: being an exile, in Weil's intention, contributes to the absence of something which is fundamental to the human soul.

Weil defines the idea of 'root' in the writings commissioned by the Free French movement for which she was working in London in 1943, later published as *L'Enracinement* in 1949 (in English as *The Need for Roots* in 1952). The report was meant to address the possibility of regeneration in France after the devastation of the war and after Germany had been defeated. The elaboration of these ideas was, therefore, chronologically parallel to her work on *Venice Saved*, which she started in 1940 but which she kept modifying until the end of her life. According to Little, '*Venise Sauvée* is but an artistic expression of the theory embodied in *L'Enracinement*' (Little 1979: 301).

The importance of roots cannot be overstated. Weil writes,

> To be rooted is perhaps the most important and least recognized need of the human soul. It is one of the hardest to define. A human being has roots by virtue of his real, active and natural participation in the life of a community which preserves in living shape certain particular treasures of the past and certain

particular expectations for the future. This participation is a natural one, in the sense that it is automatically brought about by place, conditions of birth, profession and social surroundings. Every human being needs to have multiple roots. It is necessary for him to draw wellnigh the whole of his moral, intellectual and spiritual life by way of the environment of which he forms a natural part. (NR 43)

Social, cultural, geographical contexts are not merely collateral factors in a human life. They nourish something deep in the individual, who finds not only a sense of identity but a sense of meaning and purpose through a connection with her past, her fellows and her landscape as well as – importantly – her work. We may wonder how these considerations would apply in the twenty-first century, when, in a globalized world with increasing mobility, public discourse encourages the individual to be self-sufficient and regard roots as something to be shaken off; we could also wonder what Weil's ideas on roots mean for one of the most disastrous contemporary issues, namely the situation of refugees.

Venice, the city, gives roots to its people. Therein lies its power and, to an extent, the spiritual reason for Jaffier's decision. It is more than the desire to benefit individuals: it is the recognition of what, beyond the individual, offers spiritual nourishment to the people present and to come. The conspirators, lacking roots, have substituted them with the social, thereby also giving up on higher aspirations and an independent sense of morality. Their concerns are not the concerns of the group. But, as we have seen, the group must obey its own laws (the laws of 'gravity'), which include the blind destruction of everything that is not itself, everything it cannot incorporate. This is the great opposition in the play: rootlessness against roots; gravity against human spiritual fulfilment; destruction against existence; dream against reality.

The Universal Significance of Venice Saved

These are the elements that Weil sees manifested, starkly, in the events she is portraying in the play. They are the forces that agitate underneath historical events of different eras. Weil herself draws explicit parallels between the Spanish in Venice and what the Romans did, for example, to Carthage. ('The Romans wept for Carthage, but they destroyed it', says Renaud approvingly in Act Two Scene Four.) In Weil's notes to the play we read the following:

> In the first act: the idea of Empire.
> Social without roots, social without city: the Roman Empire.
> A Roman would always think *we*.
> A Hebrew also.

Weil is showing that there is no difference between imperialistic forces when it comes to their underlying factors: uprootedness and force. The same evils are then passed on to those who are being conquered.

In the passage from Act Two quoted above, Renaud's encouraging speech to Jaffier continues by saying that the united Europe under Spanish hegemony will be 'bringing civilization and Christianity, as Spain has done for America. And all that will be thanks to you'. It is difficult not to read in these lines an ironically bitter description, not only of the fate of American populations after European invasion but also of more recent events, which Weil could possibly not foresee, but the motivating forces of which she clearly understood.

Finally, and crucially, there is the German expansion in the 1930s and 1940s, the most recent manifestation of the forces Weil depicts in her play, emerging starkly during the last years of her life, as she was Writing *Venice Saved* and *The Need for Roots*. 'The scene of Venice in 1618 is the scene of Europe in 1940', Fiori writes; 'The motivations of the mercenaries are the motivations of the Nazis. ... Venice, "the city" which represents the roots, "the contact with nature, the past, and tradition," is Europe. Over both there looms the menace of *moral decomposition*' (1989: 187–8).

It is very clear that *Venice Saved* is far from an idle exercise in fiction of an antiquarian taste. It is an urgent call to recognize and respond to the moral and spiritual perils that history has presented again and again. In the letter to Joseph-Marie Perrin later called 'Spiritual autobiography', dated 1942, Weil understands clearly that she is living in an exceptional historical era, where our obligation for the next two or three years … is to show the public the possibility of a truly incarnated Christianity. In all the history now known there has never been a period in which souls have been in such peril as they are to-day in every part of the globe. (WG 42)

Venice Saved was part of Weil's attempts to combat this peril.

Weil and the Tragic

The Tragic Form

Simone Weil's choice to write a tragedy, in the midst of the political upheaval she was witnessing, the suffering all around her, and her own uprooting and constant, intense spiritual search, is no coincidence and certainly no escapism. On the contrary, both the content and the form of tragedy perfectly suit Weil's situation and the kinds of questions she was raising elsewhere in her work. Before writing *Venice Saved*, apart from some poems Weil stuck to prose, mostly philosophical/political and aphoristic. Now she chooses to write something completely different – a play. Why this form?

In order to understand the significance of tragedy for Weil, we need to remember that her inspiration was the theatre of ancient Greece. Weil felt a particular attraction to this world, where she thought she could see early expressions of fundamental ideas of hers of Christian inspiration (some of which she also saw in Indian, Chinese and Egyptian thought) – as shown in her writings on ancient authors, collected in *Intimations of Christianity among the Ancient Greeks* (1957).

The Greek theatre, as Giancarlo Gaeta (n.d.) points out, was also a political instrument, aimed not just at the entertainment but at the education and inner purification of the citizens. It displayed stark truths about life in safer form, so that the viewer could reflect and engage emotionally, until the final *catharsis*. As Thomas Nevin observes (anticipating some key themes in this chapter), 'Not accidentally, Weil chose the most public of arts to portray the passage of the Holy Spirit through a single soul and the consequent preservation of a community' (Nevin 2000: 167).

From the Greek theatre Weil maintains not only the political but also the religious aspect, which is manifested as mystical in her work; that is, the deep awareness that the events represented have significance beyond the outward facts, that they are symbols of supernatural forces which underlie and determine human existence.

To the reader unacquainted with her thought, however, *Venice Saved* may not appear to be a work of mystical inspiration. As Thomas Nevin claims, 'The spiritual dimensions of this work are like the harmony of the spheres, not heard yet there' (2000: 167). Weil's notes, however, and some knowledge of her philosophy, make it clear that *Venice Saved* is pervaded by the supernatural. It is precisely because, according to Weil, the supernatural is present everywhere, but not normally perceived, that her representation cannot show obvious marks of it.

Weil's view of tragedy, then, is religious, and more specifically Christian. According to Katherine Brueck (1995), Weil's entire approach to literature is 'supernaturalist' and 'redemptive', something that sets Weil's play apart from much of the literature of her century, which lacks a transcendent orientation. Hers, according to Brueck, is a distinctive Christian tragedy, different not only from modernist literature but also from romanticism and even from Aristotelian theory, all of which rely on natural explanations, resolving guilt and punishment in the social and physical world. Weil's hero is not defined by the turn of events around him: his movement is all internal. Rather than remaining in the natural realm, or identifying the natural with the supernatural, Weil's hero mediates between the two (Brueck 1995: 17). From a natural perspective, there is little justice in *Venice Saved*: Jaffier betrays and is betrayed, the Venetian aristocracy turns out to be just as ruthless as the Spanish, the hero is crushed, dishonoured, he loses his one true friend and opts for a self-orchestrated death in a fight. Yet it is precisely from this that Weil's Christian tragedy derives its meaning. Justice is not to be sought in the world, but in the supernatural. Jaffier is not a hero only for saving Venice, but for his ability to see the world truly and for bearing – at least at certain moments – absolute affliction without consolation. The resolution of *Venice Saved* is the resolution of Christ's cross: truth coincides with annihilation of the self, if borne with love (see 'The Cross and Affliction' below).

Looking at the recent filmic representation of Weil's play can be instructive in learning how another reader of Weil imagined a piece that was never performed during Weil's life. Serena Nono, who directed the film *Venezia Salva* (2013) based on the play, explains how for her the Greek inspiration was fundamental to the text and it was necessary to maintain it in the film, including what she calls its 'fixedness':

> It was very important for me to focus on the form of this film concentrating on fixedness and directing the non-actors to present the essence of Weil's ideas through essential recitation, and with her stage directions. The philosopher Simone Weil conceived this play as a Greek tragedy. That is the reason I chose a classical form, and the depiction of immobility in a play where there is little action. ... Movement is all internal, not in physical actions. The idea of non-action that acts is central in *Venice Saved*. The main character converts (moves) to the idea of non-violence (non-action). (Nono n.d.)

For Weil, immobility seems to have been a standard to be applied to drama of all times. She writes, 'Only drama without movement is truly beautiful. Shakespeare's tragedies are second-class with the exception of *Lear*. Those of Racine, third-class except for *Phèdre*. Those of Corneille of the *n*th class' (GG 149). Weil writes in her notes to *Venice Saved* that Jaffier, Violetta and her father are characterized by immobility; that the second act contains the zeal of the conspiracy in opposition to Jaffier's immobility and that the third act is just 'immobility'. In a play that is fundamentally about abstract, inner and supernatural forces, action is secondary. Jaffier's conversion is not determined by events, but by 'grace'. Violetta is immobile as she is a symbol for Venice, for the beauty that takes possession of Jaffier and captures his attention. This lack of movement can also be understood, on the stage, as a visual representation of Jaffier's decreasing role in the world, his shrinking both in social role and in his self (decreation).

Antigone *and a Higher Law*

Among the Greek tragedies, Weil seemed to have a particular predilection for *Antigone* by Sophocles, composed in the fifth century BCE. Quotes from *Antigone* can be found on the front cover of two of her notebooks, and when she had the possibility to write for a workers' periodical (*Entre Nous*) she chose to write an article on *Antigone*, which was published on 16 May 1936 (see SL 49–50). Discussions of the tragedy recur in her writing, including the later *Intimations*. The 1936 article contains in condensed form Weil's interpretation of *Antigone*, showing its political relevance and introducing its metaphysical dimension, which will become more important and explicit in later writings.

The tragedy in *Antigone* is hinged on a conflict. Antigone wants to give proper burial to her brother Polynices; however, King Creon, her uncle, prohibits this, because he considers Polynices to be a traitor. Therefore, Antigone is condemned to death for her disobedience. The irreconcilable conflict occurs because Antigone and Creon do not simply disagree, but think and act according to two separate laws or worldviews. These have often been interpreted as natural law and positive law, but Weil is more radical: she sees the tragedy as arising from the juxtaposition of the natural and the supernatural: 'He judges everything from the point of view of the State; she holds to another view which seems to her superior' (IC 21). The incommensurability of the two perspectives also explains why it is possible, for the reader, to sympathize with the conspirators and disagree with Jaffier's decision to save the city. This kind of opposition is, in a sense, not really a conflict, since the natural and the supernatural are separate levels of being, not to be placed side by side.

This contrast between the natural and the supernatural, together with the importance of obeying the latter, is central to Weil's thought and emerges clearly in *Venice Saved* as well. Jaffier can be compared to Antigone, acting out of obedience to a higher order which is, because of its very nature, incomprehensible to the Creon characters (Renaud and the Secretary of the Council of Ten). In her play, Weil stresses this 'worldly', natural perspective, and how it is held up exactly in the same way by both the conspirators and the Venetians, in two speeches, one by Renaud and one by the Secretary, meant to be 'lessons in high politics', yet proving to be nothing but the ruthless and expansionist discourse of force (Act Two Scene Six).

The political intent of Weil's *Entre Nous* essay on *Antigone* is clear from the contrast between Antigone and her sister Ismene, meek and obedient to those in power, unwilling to rebel and face the consequences. For Weil, the workers can aspire to be like Antigone:

to have the courage, despite their miserable conditions and their oppression, to maintain a truthful vision of reality and inner freedom (Cabaud Meaney 2007: 82). Jaffier's example can also be understood as Weil's hope that those who were experiencing the dramatic turns of events of the Second World War would hold on to fundamental moral values, instead of yielding to unjust albeit easier courses of action out of fear or submission to power.

Marie Cabaud Meaney observes how Weil's times needed, like perhaps no other, this kind of reflection, when people were faced with what seemed like impossible choices:

> Those who avoided a difficult choice and closed their eyes often became collaborators with totalitarian systems, while others, who refused to avert their eyes, frequently had to die as witnesses to truth, justice, and God. Adopting a purely natural point of view could not guarantee the clarity of vision needed to see through the lies of power and ideology. (2007: 77–8)

Decreation

But, as we are beginning to see, the political theme, which Weil observed behind *Antigone* and her own play, needs to be understood on the basis of Weil's religious metaphysics. What follows is a brief summary.

Weil starts from the premise that God is fullness of being. If that is so, however, God cannot coexist with anything else. This poses the problem of God in the created world, which is not identical with God. The solution, for Weil, lies in a 'withdrawal' of God, in a supreme act of love, to allow the world to exist. (These ideas are present in the Kabbalistic tradition of Isaac Luria, where God's withdrawal is known as *tzimtzum*.) (See Chapter 4.) However, because everything emanates from the act of an absent God, reality is both empty of divinity and also bears its mark. God is present through God's absence, like the wall separating two prisoners in their cells, which at the same time acts as their means of communication with each other (GG 145).

This sketch of Weil's metaphysics is important for our purposes because from it are derived several key ideas and concepts, which allow us to see what is really happening in *Venice Saved*, even when the play seems puzzling. To begin with, if creation tears God apart from God, creating in being a 'region of opacity' (Vetö 1994: 5), it means that fullness of God can only be restored when creation returns to nothing. Everything in creation obeys laws of necessity for Weil, except for one thing: the autonomous will. In being created, a creature accepts its own existence and therefore God's self-laceration, preferring itself to God. This is sin and evil (cf. Vetö 1994: 16). It is not that creatures can choose not to obey God's necessity, but they can rebel against it through their will. As Weil puts it, 'A creature cannot but obey. The only choice given to men, as intelligent and free creatures, is to desire obedience or not to desire it' (IC 186). Desiring to obey equals renouncing one's will.

If 'evil is the distance between the creature and God' (NB 342), the good consists in trying to bridge the distance. For Weil, this is decreation (*décreation*): to give up the only element in the whole of creation which is able to be discordant from God – the will, including all ego and everything that is 'personal' – thus partially mending the tear. By giving up our will in obedience, we give up ourselves, and at the same time give our consent to reality as God has ordered it. 'To live while ceasing to exist so that in a self that is no longer the self God and his creation may find themselves face to face' (NB 464). This would parallel God's creative, self-denying act, which is the supreme act of love.[1]

Decreation, then, is an integral aspect of Weil's moral and metaphysical thought, and it is necessary for us if we are to avoid sin. In action, this resolves itself as not choosing out of personal will, but allowing oneself to be guided by reality – which partakes, in a world reverberating with God, of the supernatural. This is the task of *attention*, which Weil defines thus:

> Attention consists of suspending our thought, leaving it detached, empty and ready to be penetrated by the object. ... Above all our thought should be empty, waiting, not seeking anything, but ready to receive in its naked truth the object which is to penetrate it. (WG 72)

Returning to the two tragedies we have been examining, decreation through attention is what leads both Antigone, in Weil's interpretation, and Jaffier to act against authority and to face its terrible consequences. Antigone obeys a law that is supernatural, and on account of that quality it is both irreconcilable with positive law and, once seen, impossible to disobey. If the true good resides, as Weil thought, in the realm of the supernatural, then doing anything else but what the supernatural requires by conforming to worldly rules would be evil. As Weil starkly puts it, 'In all the crucial problems of human existence the only choice is between supernatural good on the one hand and evil on the other' (Weil in Miles 2005: 86).

Jaffier, similarly, in moments of increasing stillness, which seem to signify increasing 'decreation' through abandonment of personal will, comes to realize that the destruction of Venice (which would be the epitome of the assertion of a personal will) is not just wrong, but *impossible*. As Jaffier says, in a statement that for Weil is quite literally true, although that's not how he means it: 'this beauty will be mine – impossible!' Jaffier pays attention to Venice, to the beauty and the reality of it, and is unable to carry out the plan. Similarly, Rees notes, 'Jaffier is not a free agent. Once the supernatural has taken possession of him he has no choice but to act as he does' (1958: 203).

Weil asks, 'In which cases does the struggle against temptation exhaust the energy attached to goodness and in which cases does it make it rise higher in the scale of qualities of energy?' The answer: 'This must depend on the respective importance of the parts played by the will and the attention' (GG 43). Jaffier pays attention. Attention means renouncing the will. What happens then is the result of obedience.

> We should not take one step, *even in the direction of what is good*, beyond that to which we are irresistibly impelled by God, and this applies to action, word and thought. But we should be willing to go anywhere under his impulsion, even to the farthest limit (the cross). ... To be willing to go as far as possible is to pray to be impelled, but without knowing whither. (GG 44)

As Weil writes in 'Human Personality', one of her most highly regarded essays, it is not the idea of rights that stops us from committing crimes nor is it anything personal about individuals that refrains us from harming them. It is something deeper – their whole being, their soul – which cries out for justice. Not, however, the justice of a court of law, but the higher justice, pertaining to truths which are objective and eternal: 'The word justice means two very different things according to whether it refers to the one or the other level. It is only the former [eternal] one that matters' (Weil in Miles 2005: 72). As Jaffier and Antigone find out, obeying the higher law is not an easy matter. Because there is no room for it in the world in which they live, their conversion means their destruction: 'Those who share only in love and not in hate belong to another world and have nothing to expect from this world but a violent death' (NR 9).

Jaffier is able to obey the order of the world because he is alone. Though leading the conspiracy, he nonetheless never lets himself become absorbed by the group, the 'social':

> Impersonality is only reached by the practice of a form of attention which is rare in itself and impossible except in solitude; and not only physical but mental solitude. This is never achieved by a man who thinks of himself as a member of a collectivity, as part of something which says 'We'. (Weil in Miles 2005: 76)

This is how Jaffier is able to pay attention, to see Venice and become aware of its existence, and then be led by the irresistible course of obedience. 'As soon as Jaffier realizes that Venice *exists* ...', Weil writes in her notes. She continues, 'To believe in the reality of the external world and to love it: one and the same thing'.

Love is attention to the real. Through attention, we enable reality to impress itself upon us. Then the facts become internally motivating, and action follows. The awareness of the existence of something else, not to speak of someone else, is incredibly difficult, according to Weil, because we naturally tend to project ourselves – our ego, will, fantasies – upon reality. This is what she calls the 'imagination', a self-driven, de-realizing force. Imagination and attention are opposites. One leads away from truth, the other towards it. But for pure truth to be manifest, efforts of attention are not sufficient. One needs grace, and that is what descends on Jaffier when contemplating Venice. (See his very poignant lines about preserving Venice in Act Two Scene Thirteen.)

By contrast, the conspirators, blindly following the laws of necessity, continually project their own will upon the world, excluding the existence of everything outside themselves. That is why they are repeatedly described – even by themselves – as 'dreamers', a usually gentle word that in Weil's context takes on very sinister significance. Renaud is clear on this, and on the violent upshot of the dream: 'Yes, we are dreaming. Men of action and enterprise are dreamers; they prefer dream to reality. But they use arms to make others dream their dreams' (Act Two Scene Six). In 'Human Personality', Weil explains the attractiveness of this phenomenon:

> There are no other restraints upon our will than material necessity and the existence of other human beings around us. Any imaginary extension of these limits is seductive, so there is a seduction in whatever helps us to forget the reality of the obstacles. That is why upheavals like war and civil war are so intoxicating; they empty human lives of their reality and seem to turn people into puppets. That is also why slavery is so pleasant to the masters. (Weil in Miles 2005: 72)

And that is why the dream of conquest was so pleasant to Renaud. Jaffier's role is to destroy the dream and bring reality, even for a moment.

Beauty

What brings about Jaffier's conversion is the realization that Venice exists. This change is described as accompanied by a sentiment of pity and led by the awareness of Venice's beauty. Pity for the beauty of a city, rather than for the horrors its inhabitants would undergo? Indeed. If this seems odd, reading Weil's essay 'Love of the Order of the World' (WG 113–35), together with her thoughts on detachment, may help us somewhat.

Weil holds that beauty is one of the keys to the supernatural. It is one of the 'forms of the implicit love of God' (WG 94–166) and takes a special place among the other forms because of its accessibility to human nature. The beautiful for Weil is the order of the world when it is loved. Beauty does not have an objective existence separate from our perception of it, but, being created by God, it manifests itself to our observation when we are loving or attentive (WG 119, 125).

Unlike the other two forms of implicit love that Weil presents before this one, beauty is relatively accessible to the imperfect intellect of human beings. Loving our neighbour is extremely hard, and so is the love of religious practices. But beauty offers itself to us and stimulates in us a response. This response is desire, which Weil sees as normally destructive and dangerous, but beauty has a trick: it stimulates desire but deflects possession, because it is in its nature that it cannot be owned. The beautiful is always distant, separate. Through this structure, beautiful things accomplish the most important task of all: to stimulate love and attention and to discourage the imagination (which in Weil's sense is possessive and distortive), thus providing an entry into the truly beautiful: the universe as a whole, or the order of the world. If the order of the world is the truly beautiful, then beauty and truth are the same. (See Weil in Miles 2005: 93.) When we fully understand something's beauty, we also respect its reality. This is what Jaffier does. Beauty, Dostoevsky's Prince Myshkin is reported to have said, will save the world. In Weil's story it saved Venice.

Weil expresses these ideas in a beautiful passage from 'Human Personality' which is worth quoting in full:

> Beauty is the supreme mystery of this world. It is a gleam which attracts the attention and yet does nothing to sustain it. Beauty always promises, but never gives anything; it stimulates hunger but has no nourishment for the part of the soul which looks in this world for sustenance. It feeds only the part of the soul that gazes. While exciting desire, it makes clear that there is nothing in it to be desired, because the one thing we want is that it should not change. If one does not seek means to evade the exquisite anguish it inflicts, then desire is gradually transformed into love; and one begins to acquire the faculty of pure and disinterested attention. (Weil in Miles 2005: 92)

To sustain an impossible desire is the possibility afforded by beauty, more easily than by love of other people. In fact, Weil thought that in her time it was beauty which could offer some salvation

> at the present time, in the countries of the white races, the beauty of the world is almost the only way by which we allow God to penetrate us, for we are still further removed from the other two [love of neighbour and of religious practices]. (WG 117–8)

Jaffier's access to the supernatural occurs though contemplation of beauty – not of the people and the fate awaiting them, because attending to people is much harder. However, the Venetians are not excluded by this contemplation, because they are part of the order of the world represented by beauty, and because Venice is what gives them roots and nourishes their soul.

The moment of recognition of beauty is a moment of detachment. Pity, which is Jaffier's motive for the betrayal, as Weil stresses, stems from his recognition of the reality of Venice. Such recognition means that, like in the contemplation of beauty, there is no attachment in pity. Pity is only possible when the self is empty and has given up all desires, which are by their nature self-serving. Pity, attention and love go hand in hand

> to empty ourselves of false divinity. … Such consent is love. The face of this love turned to thinking persons is love of neighbour. The face turned toward matter is love of the order of the world or the love of beauty which is the same thing. (WG 115)

Therefore, Jaffier's detachment, perceived in the tragedy, is real, but it should not be read as mere aesthetic appreciation combined with indifference to the inhabitants of the city. His detachment is part of his decreative moment, which is what enables him to see reality and thus transcend the natural order, with all its violence determined by necessity and gravity. If we find it difficult to understand or sympathize, that is quite natural: Jaffier's retreat, as Weil writes, is supernatural.

Friendship

The tragic contrast in Weil's play has been described above as a contrast between worldly law and supernatural law, representing two levels of reality on which the characters move, Jaffier on the latter, everyone else on the former. (With the significant and rather disappointing exception, as discussed in Chapter 1, of Violetta, the main female character, who is too stereotyped and flat to be taken seriously as a character, rather than the embodiment of an idea.) This split animates the plot and drives the whole story, enabling Weil to give dramatic representation to her notions of beauty, attention, affliction and so on. This deep meaning of the play, however, does not exhaust the oppositions manifested in the tragic action. There is another, apparently more ordinary theme, which is worth examining through Weil's characteristically non-ordinary ideas: the betrayal of friendship.

The friendship between Pierre and Jaffier is repeatedly stressed in the play, with entire conversations revolving around this topic, the two friends frequently expressing the depth of their feelings for each other, and Jaffier's thoughts returning again and again to Pierre when he knows he has been arrested, while Pierre continues to profess loyalty and friendship for him. Friendship for Pierre is the reason Jaffier entered the conspiracy and, ironically, it is Pierre who persuades Renaud that Jaffier is worthy of leading the attack. Power attracts them, but for both Pierre and Jaffier, their friendship is more important.

Friendship has a special place in Weil's thought. In her discussion of the forms of implicit love of God, friendship is treated after love of one's neighbour, of religious ceremonies and of the beauty of the world (in WG). After discussing forms of love that are impersonal, Weil considers a type of relationship that we would, normally, regard as the opposite of impersonal. And yet 'There is … a personal and human love which is pure and which enshrines an intimation and a reflection of divine love. This is friendship' (WG 152). Weil even interprets Christ's command to 'love one another' as a command to form the bond of friendship. Every other personal bond, for her, could be impure and tainted by attachment. Only friendship allows the coexistence of personal existence with something higher.

The value of friendship for Weil consists in the fact that, in its pure form, it allows the union of necessity (of which we are part, given our creaturely condition) and liberty (the only element which is not entirely bound by deterministic laws). In ordinary human relationships, we hamper liberty either through attachment or through the desire to please. In both cases, the faculty of free consent is denied, in the other or in oneself. It is very difficult indeed not to ignore or suppress free consent in the other, through need, attachment and fantasy. This is one way in which we de-realize others, ignore or distort their reality. Instead, appreciating someone else's existence, for Weil, is nothing else but pure and supernatural love (GG 64). True friendship is, likewise, impersonal and thus supernatural. (These reflections on friendship can be found in WG 152–60).

Based on this, the friendship between Jaffier and Pierre becomes far more than a plot device. It is, first, an intimation of the fact that Jaffier is capable of detachment and therefore of attention to a reality that lies beyond the world of the deeds he is engaged in. Second, it provides a perfect completion to Jaffier's affliction at the end. Being betrayed by the Venetians, insulted, despised, exiled, knowing that his actions led to the death of many people was not sufficient. With the loss of his friend, Jaffier's afflicted state is truly complete.

The Cross and Affliction

We mentioned at the start of this chapter that Weil's reading of the Greek classics, and her general spiritual outlook, is of a Christian kind. The image that best condenses her tragic thought, her notion of decreation and indeed her whole religious metaphysics, is Christ on the cross.

The cross for Weil represents the moment of absolute truth through a rare and extraordinary human experience: affliction. She writes,

In the realm of suffering, affliction is something apart, specific and irreducible. It is quite a different thing from simple suffering. It takes possession of the soul and marks it through and through with its own particular mark, the mark of slavery. (WG 76)

Affliction is different from suffering in intensity and in kind. Suffering allows some possibility of selfhood because it does not destroy the sufferer completely; in suffering there is still some hope or consolation, even in the form of self-pity. Affliction is absolute: one is destroyed in one's deepest being and loses part of one's soul. There is no room for hope nor for love. As affliction is total, it involves not only physical suffering but social and psychological as well. It is important for Weil that all of these aspects are present. Then there is nothing left in the individual.

Affliction is something that Weil encountered in her own life. The link between affliction and truth is also part of her experience: it was during a violent attack of headache in Solesmes, while she tried desperately to keep her attention focused on the love of God, that she felt Christ 'taking possession' of her (WG 34–5). Previously, her factory work had made her experience 'the affliction of social degradation', during which she felt like a slave 'in the Roman sense of the word' (Weil in Miles 2005: 282). (See Chapter 1.)

Venezia Salva director Serena Nono has appreciated the importance of fully understanding affliction, which is evident from her choice of collaborators for her film (2013), many of them being residents of the Casa dell'Ospitalità di Venezia e Mestre, a centre for homeless people. As she explains, 'People who live on the edge of society, who are exiles ... can easily relate to Simone Weil's idea: truth is in pain, in misfortune; truth is in beauty' (Nono, n.d.).

In affliction love, including love of God, becomes impossible. And that is precisely the point where the fate of the afflicted soul is decided. If one gives up loving in affliction, God's absence becomes irreparable. If, on the other hand, the afflicted is able to continue loving, then she is united with God: the destruction of her self is a *decreation* which allows her to restore the unity of the divine.

This impossible love is what Christ, even in the midst of extreme pain and desperation, even after crying out to God 'why did you abandon me?', was capable of. That's why the cross, for Weil, is the symbol of true Christianity. In a letter to Joseph-Marie Perrin, she states that the greatest privilege for her would be to take the place of the good thief, sharing in Christ's affliction which was at the same time his glorification (WG 26).

Antigone, too, in Weil's eyes, is capable of holding on to her conviction and the love of the good and of the gods even before being buried alive, completely defeated in the eyes of the world. Cabaud Meaney (2007) talks of Antigone's 'Passion', 'since she experiences an abandonment similar to that of Christ on the cross', in moments of clear affliction that Weil refers to more than once, including in her article on *Entre Nous*. Antigone appears here 'emptied of all security and self-regard'. Yet it is in this emptiness, together with her love, 'extreme and apparently absurd', that Antigone is able to stop the curse – just as Christ can redeem the sins of humanity (Cabaud Meaney 2007: 91).

Jaffier is an afflicted man. Weil makes it clear, repeating the word 'affliction' (*malheur*) and its cognates several times in the play. Jaffier is a traitor, he is betrayed, he knows his friend is being tortured, and even the Venetians, instead of feeling grateful to him, despise him. The last outcome is no surprise: Weil knew very well that few things are as hard as to love the afflicted.

Jaffier's monologue of affliction in Act Three was clearly one of the tragedy's key points for Weil, and it appears that she drafted around fifty different versions of it (Campo 1987: 18). Jaffier is now in the position he was going to place the people of Venice in: he lacks reality. He asks himself, 'Do I exist?'. The afflicted man loses everything, including his existence. And then, 'Have I been transformed into an animal?'. The respect which he thought was owed to a human being is not given to him. Here we are also reminded of something particularly poignant today: non-human animals are in our society widely treated as mere things, all inner and outer life taken away from them, in countless 'farms' and laboratories around the world. With this in mind, we can see Jaffier's animal-like treatment as a yet more extreme form of affliction.

Jaffier goes through different phases in his monologue. He tries to communicate and no one answers him; he tries to flatter and persuade; he seeks material comfort in food and sleep; he pities himself; he rebels; then he surrenders and becomes very still. When the torture of his friends is over, he utters 'it is finished', reminiscent of Christ's final words on the cross.

Did Jaffier achieve contact with absolute good, with God? Did he manage to love the real in the midst of affliction? The reader may answer for herself, bearing in mind that Weil may have provided a clearer answer had she finished the play. What we know is that Weil portrayed a man captured by beauty and decreated by affliction, and that both were ways of reaching the realm of the absolute, which is humanity's task always, but perhaps yet more pressing in difficult times like the 1940s.

> We know then that joy is the sweetness of contact with the love of God, that affliction is the wound of this same contact when it is painful, and that only the contact matters, not the manner of it. (WG 53)

On the Translation

Venice Saved *and Translation*

Simone Weil's *Venise Sauvée*, together with relevant paratextual material by her, was first published by Gallimard in 1955 and again in 1968 as part of an edition that also includes ten poems, a fairy-tale she wrote as a child and a letter about her poetry from Paul Valéry, entitled *Poèmes suivis de Venise Sauvée, Lettre de Paul Valéry* (Poems followed by *Venice Saved*, Letter from Paul Valéry). Weil's poetry and the play together form the forthcoming *Tome 3* of the *Œuvres Complètes*, that is, the fifth volume in the series. We have used the 1968 edition as a basis for this first published English translation. A translation and adaptation by Richard Rees was broadcast on BBC radio in January 1957, but never appeared in print. Weil's play was first performed in French by the Théâtre Universitaire de Marseille (University Theatre of Marseilles) in 1965. There is an Italian translation, *Venezia Salva* (*Venice Saved*), by Cristina Campo (1987) and a film of that translation by Serena Nono (2013). Readers without French or Italian therefore have no access to this work, so that the primary purpose of our translation is to open up new possibilities of encountering Weil.

When Ludwig Wittgenstein became involved in C. K. Ogden's English translation of his 1921 *Tractatus Logico-Philosophicus*, he remarked about translation: 'It *is* a difficult business!' (1973: 19). And that is the great surprise. Translation ought to be easy. If you can speak a language and if you can use a dictionary, then surely you can translate. David Bellos (2018), however, argues that things are rarely so simple. In a discussion of the Maigret detective novels of Georges Simenon, he recounts how the stylistic simplicity of the stories might lead a reader to think that the work is easy to translate, but goes on:

> There is no perfect way of translating Maigret. ... The relative difficulty of a translation task, it seems to me, does not arise from the value or importance of the original, but from the

nature of written language, from the passing of time, and from the lack of a neat fit between the cultures of source and target. (2018: 65)

Translation is never a case of simply transferring content, despite the etymology of the work being 'to carry across'. The reason for this is that many texts – especially literary texts – are about more than the communication of ideas. Terry Eagleton makes the point in a discussion of poetry, but it holds for all language that exhibits literariness:

People sometimes talk about digging out the ideas 'behind' the poem's language, but this spatial metaphor is misleading … the language of the poem is *constitutive* of its ideas. (2007: 2)

Literary translation must be more than a leap from dictionary to dictionary: it must be a reimagining, as Eliot Weinberger stresses (Weinberger and Paz 1987: 34). There will always be more than one way of translating a literary work. Translations will differ according to time and place and author. Michael Hamburger writes about his versions of the German poet Friedrich Hölderlin: 'No translation can be definitive, if only because it remains one person's rendering of what he or she has made of the words read' (2007: xxvi). There is no notion of natural equivalence to which the translator can appeal, because the meaning of a word will vary depending on how it is used, as Wittgenstein points out in *Philosophical Investigations* 43. Even if some features (such as stage directions or a particular number of syllables in a particular line) can be maintained, the translation of literature is ultimately transformative.

A creative response is thus demanded of the translators of *Venice Saved*, given that the play is literary in nature: it aims to produce poetic and dramatic effects on its readers, rather than to inform us about the details of a failed Spanish conspiracy in Venice in 1618. In any case, Weil has placed her own spin on the events narrated by Saint-Réal, just as the other writers who have used this source, so that it would be a category error to read the play in order to be informed about Venetian history. (See Chapter 2.)

We have argued that the twenty-first-century reader of *Venice Saved* needs background about the life and thought of Weil if she is to appreciate the play. Similarly, the reader for translation needs to reconstruct the beliefs and attitudes of the writer of the source text (Boase-Beier 2015: 21), because all texts come out of what Wittgenstein would call 'forms of life' (*Investigations* 241). Research into such forms of life is necessary. By seeking to understand the context, culture and ways of seeing the world that shape any source text, 'translation becomes anthropology' (Wilson 2016: 42).

How then can *Venice Saved* be reimagined in English? The title itself causes problems, because Otway's tragedy *Venice Preserv'd* is known in French as *Venise Sauvée*, which Weil also called her play in what we can infer to be a conscious nod to a work that had made a big impact in French Literature. (In Balzac's 1835 novel *Père Goriot*, for example, one of the characters tells another that he knows *Venise Sauvée* by heart (1966: 155).) By translating the title as *Venice Saved*, we show that we are dealing with difference as well as similarity, and that this translation is a new creation. The lexical space of a 'preserved' Venice has been taken; translation in this case moves the title to new lexical space.

All translation begins with this activity of reading for translation. Weil's play is competently written in imitation of classical models – we are at times in the world of Racine – and the translation imitates this formalism. Some characters speak in syllabic verse at times of heightened emotions: Jaffier after he has betrayed the conspiracy; Renaud and Pierre as they face torture and execution; the apprentice as he threatens Jaffier in the name of Venice. (Most of Act Three is in verse, and Weil's notes indicate that she intended to incorporate more verse earlier in the play.) Many poetic works, such as Homer's *Iliad*, have at times been translated into prose, but Weil's differentiation between poetry and prose makes a literary point and the distinction for us was worth preserving. Richard O'Brien argues that if we set aside our preoccupations, then verse drama can be seen as

a form surprisingly well-suited to exploring some of our most pressing contemporary questions. How can we share our world? How can we talk across divides? Who is taking up space in the conversation, who is muscled out, and how can they push back?

(2018: 24)

Such questions are at the heart of *Venice Saved*.

The play ends with a lyric poem in which Violetta salutes a new dawn over the saved city, even though she is herself ignorant of how close Venice came to disaster. We aim to recreate the lyricism, which involved imitating the stanzas of the source text and using slant line where Weil uses full rhyme. Violetta symbolizes the beauty of Venice, the beauty that moves Jaffier to pity and causes him to betray his friends and to cast his own soul into affliction. Hence her language should show (by its form) her vision of a transcendent reality to which, as Weil believes, we can have access through attention.

Is the play more than just competent? What are its literary merits? In 1937, Weil sent her poem 'Prométhée' (Prometheus) to Valéry, a poet whom she admired, asking his opinion. In his reply, Valéry states that the poem is well made, though he criticizes a number of lines and sees a heaviness in the syllabic verse. He notes that 'the poem is a bit too noticeably "didactic". … It is too informative' (PVS 9; our translation). He concludes his letter by praising:

A *will of composition*, to which I attach the greatest importance in view of the rarity of this concern in poetry.
Concern is not the right word. By composition, I understand something other than the logical or chronological order that flows from a subject. I am thinking of a much subtler quality, the rarest that there is and, which the greatest poets have generally overlooked. (PVS 10; our translation)

We catch in the letter the voice of the creative writing teacher to the capable but overenthusiastic student: show, don't tell, but hang on to what you are doing well. Valéry's comments could be applied to *Venice Saved*.

The temptation to improve upon Weil's work has been resisted. There is a static nature to the play; it can be regarded as a closet drama that looks back in time and is a world away from the sort of play that would come to dominate the French stage after the Second World War, such as *Waiting for Godot* by Samuel Beckett or *Rhinoceros* by Eugène Ionesco. Translation is a way of reading that foregrounds both literariness and the lack of literariness. In any case, we should never forget that the play is unfinished. If Weil had lived, who knows what might have happened?

We argued above that there is no notion of natural equivalence to which translators can appeal. However, when it comes to the translation of philosophy, some words do have 'equivalents' that have been *constructed* by tradition, as argued by Duncan Large (2019). Thus, terms such as Plato's 'Forms' or Kant's 'categorical imperative' are consistently used in Anglophone philosophy. Some words are even left in the source language; Heidegger's *Dasein*, for example, is routinely kept in German, because Heidegger means more than just 'being' by this noun. With Weil, a case in point is the noun *malheur*, which might be translated as 'unhappiness' in other contexts. In her work, however, the word holds a particular resonance, indicating a higher state of suffering that can take us to God, just as Christ was afflicted on the cross (see GG 72–6). Weil's translators have chosen to translate *malheur* as 'affliction' and we follow this construct; in Act Three Scene Four, for example, Jaffier calls himself 'Malheureux!', and we translate this as 'Afflicted man!', allowing the word in the source text to foreground Weil's unique understanding of suffering in translation by relating it intertextually to her work as a whole. Philosophical terms have no meaning in themselves, only relative to a theory. Similarly, Weil uses the noun 'L'enracinement' (rootedness) in her comments on the play, which is the French title of *The Need for Roots* (2002a). Images of rootedness and uprooting are found in both paratext and text. Here we translate 'L'enracinement' as 'Being rooted' because that phrase fits the sentence's grammar better, and we clarify the intertextual situation in endnote.

Languages differ from each other not in what they may say, but in what they must say, as Roman Jakobson argues (2012: 129). French is a gendered language, so that the play's title *Venise Sauvée* marks the city as feminine by the addition of terminal *-e* to the adjective *sauvé*, something impossible to imitate in English, where adjectives do not decline. We can only reinforce the feminine imagery associated with the city throughout the play – such as it being the 'spouse' of the sea in Violetta's closing speech – and use a feminine pronoun when referring to Venice. Similarly, classical French verse works very differently from classical English verse, being based on the number and pattern of syllables in a line, rather than the number and pattern of stresses. We use the same number of syllables that Weil did in her verse (though without any attempt to duplicate any pattern of internal division) to signal that we are offering a representation of a very different way of writing poetry.

But should not a translation aim to read easily, to be fluent, to look as if it were written in the target language? Reviewers often praise 'elegant' translations. Many literary authors, however, succeed precisely because they push against the boundaries of language, writing texts that are anything but fluent. Poetry itself is typically a form of heightened (and often patterned) language. David Constantine thus argues that the way of domestication in translation is misguided, because the language of poetry should always carry with it some feeling of 'coming from abroad' (2004: 24). (His comments also apply to expressive prose.) He continues,

> For every reader some such shock of foreignness is salutary, and poetry has the power to issue it. And for the nation, especially if that nation is English-speaking, the continual shock of the foreign is absolutely indispensable. (Ibid.)

Our translation is written to preserve this shock of the foreign. Writing in 2018, at the time of Brexit, it is worth remembering in how we translate that nobody is an island.

Simone Weil and Translation

Jonathan Rée notes that 'no bookshelves are more heavily stocked with foreign books and translations than those of the philosopher' (2001: 231) and that 'European philosophy has always been written with several languages in mind; and it has to be read, and translated, with multilingual eyes as well' (2001: 235). It is worth considering translation from a philosophical perspective, as is increasingly done in the scholarly world (see Rawling and Wilson 2019), and we can use the work of Weil herself as a way in.

Weil does not address translation directly at any length in her writings, but like many philosophers sometimes refers to it obliquely as part of her general philosophical enquiry, in order to illustrate a philosophical point. She remarks, for example, on the need to 'write like a translator, and to act in the same way' (NB 215). We can investigate both aspects of this aphorism: writing like a translator and acting like a translator.

To write like a translator involves writing creatively within constraints (Boase-Beier and Holman 1999), because any translator is trying to represent what somebody has already represented. In creating *Venice Saved*, Weil was translating a prose source text (Saint-Réal) into a verse drama. A constraint upon Weil, however, remains the framework of her source. She follows the order of events described by Saint-Réal, ending the play with the downfall of the conspiracy. Yet her own philosophical framework becomes part of the literary project, as argued above: she highlights the horrors that face the civilian population should the conspiracy succeed; she shows Jaffier driven to betray his friends by pity; she makes these events a parable for issues of rootedness and affliction; she shows the role of beauty in the world. The interlingual translation must in turn show what Weil has achieved.

What characterizes living as a translator? Translators find themselves in the situation of the mediator, of occupying the middle ground, looking at both source and target texts. The middle ground, *metaxu* in Greek, is an important notion for Weil (GG 145–7) and is referred to in her notes on *Venice Saved*. (See endnote [6].) Can we take the translator to be a mediating figure between two languages? What would that involve? Weil, writing about creation, states, 'We have got to imitate the act of creating, and there are two possible ways of imitating it – the first one real, the second one apparent: by preservation and by destruction' (NB 183). Translation is always about preservation. All translators choose aspects of the source text that they feel that they must recreate. All translators regret aspects of the source text that they were not able to recreate. Translation is about choice, an informed choice based on a reading of the source text in its context. Sometimes one choice may block others, and there is destruction.

It is interesting to compare Weil with her German contemporary Walter Benjamin (1882–1940). Both were Jewish intellectuals of the left; both actively opposed Nazism; both were brought to premature deaths by the course of history, with Benjamin committing suicide to avoid being sent back to Germany, and Weil starving herself to death in exile; both developed metaphysical views that parallel the Kabbalah, an esoteric tradition of Jewish thought. Benjamin uses imagery from the Lurianic Kabbalah in his often-cited essay 'The Translator's Task':

> Just as fragments of a vessel, in order to be fitted together, must correspond to each other, so translation, instead of making itself resemble the sense of the original, must fashion its own language, carefully and in detail, a counterpart to the original's mode of meaning, in order to make both of them recognisable as fragments of a vessel, as fragments of a greater language. (2012: 81)

Translation for Benjamin is not a matter of discovering equivalences, but of matching broken pieces, in a recognition that we are working within the framework of language itself. His view is in line with the Kabbalistic belief that the holiness of texts lies in their potential for transformation (Scholem 1996: 12). The process of translation is one of attention, a point frequently made by poets about their craft, as Philip Gross notes, 'We need the writing form that specializes in the writing-in of spaciousness, of quiet calm attention as patient as birdwatchers in a hide among wide marshes' (2018: 12). Here in Benjamin is a parallel with the stress on attention of Weil, who both compared herself to a broken vessel in need of repair, as her niece Sylvie Weil records (2009: 37) and uses this image in her theory of decreation. (For the parallels between Weil and Isaac Luria's Kabbalistic thought, see McCullough (2014: 87).)

Weil herself took on the translator's task. She translated various classical texts, including lines from Homer's *Iliad* for her essay on that epic (IP 2005). She explains her strategy in the French text:

> The translation of the cited passages is new. Each line translates a Greek line, and the enjambments are scrupulously reproduced; the order of the Greek words within each line is respected as much as possible. (O 529n; our translation)

Simone Pétrement asserts, 'I believe that never before has a translation so completely captured the human tenderness and pity that pervades the *Iliad*' (1976: 362).

Further research is thus called for on the links between Benjamin and Weil; how Weil's work on attention can be used by literary theorists and by translation theorists; Weil and the Kabbalah; Weil as translator and poet. Her poems are unavailable in English translation, although they clearly mattered to her, as illustrated by her letter to Valéry, by her disappointment that Valéry did not seek a meeting with her to discuss things further and by a letter to her parents in January 1943 in which she writes that it would be 'nice to produce ... a few copies of the collection of poems', which would include Violetta's greeting of the dawn and Jaffier's last four lines (SL 168). By investigating new aspects of Weil, we can come to understand better the philosopher whose view of the world continues to intrigue readers, who developed an alternative and unique vision of the world and who wrote a play that manifests that vision and in which Venice is saved.

We hope that this first published translation in English will bring new readers to Weil, will show new aspects of her to those who have already read her work and will encourage all readers to explore further her writings on philosophy, politics and religion. We hope that we have saved what is interesting about *Venise Sauvée* and that *Venice Saved* will support what Benjamin calls the 'afterlife' of the text (2012: 76).

Venice Saved

Tragedy in Three Acts

Simone Weil

Simone Weil's Notes on *Venice Saved* [1]¹

First part of the first act. A joyful zeal for conquest. A scene with everybody saying: 'How could I have ever imagined this, when things were going so badly … ? And yet, I always did think that fate owed me a favour, which had to come sooner or later, and that I should not die before it came.'

Make them as sympathetic as possible. The spectator is to desire the success of the enterprise. Until Renaud's speech, which should have the same effect on the spectator as it has on Jaffier.

*

From the play's first lines, the *peace* of Venice should be evoked, and Venice's ignorance of what awaits.

*

In the first act – and in the second – it must be apparent that this is a conspiracy of exiles, of uprooted men.

They all hate the Venetians for having a home – apart from Jaffier. (Yes, even Pierre.)

Disgust at a monotonous existence is the motivation for the background. Evoke the boredom.

*

In the first act: the idea of Empire.

Social without roots, social without city: the Roman Empire. [2]

A Roman would always think *we*.

A Hebrew also.

Spain: the conspiracy is something *social* for the conspirators. Venice is a city.

'City' does not evoke the social.

Having roots is something different from the social. [3]

*

Jaffier. Passion. One of the meanings of passion is perhaps that all the pain, the shame and the death that you do not want to inflict on others will fall on you, without you having wished for it. As if, mathematically, affliction [4] had to compensate for distant crimes, so that the soul might stay under the power of evil (but in a different sense); reciprocally, virtue consists in keeping to oneself the evil that is suffered, in not freeing oneself from it by expelling it, by deeds or by the imagination. (Accepting the void.)

Being pure = invariance.

*

Affliction destroys the ego. It destroys part of reality, diminishes the reality of the world. Plunges into nightmare. But the corresponding action also transmutes reality into dream.

Is there a law of analogy between the two goals of a bad action, in the sense that it does analogous harm to the person who commits it and to the person who submits to it?

And is the same true for the good action?

Action would be like a language. Like works of art and so on.

Something is communicated by an action.

This can be seen in *Venice Saved*.

*

Jaffier. It is necessary to give form to the sentiment that it is the good that is abnormal. And this is how things are in this world. We do not realize this; art makes us aware of it. Abnormal but possible: this is the good.

Evil should also be shown to be vulgar, monotonous, dismal and boring.

*

Things in the form of values are unreal for us. Yet false values also remove reality from perception itself by means of the imagination that envelops it: for values are not deduced, but directly read in the sensation to which they are linked.

Thus perfect detachment alone allows us to see the nakedness of things, without the fog of lying values. This is why it was necessary for Job to suffer boils and the dung heap: so that the beauty of the world could be revealed to him. [5] For there is no detachment without pain. And there is no pain that can be borne without hatred and lies unless there is detachment.

(*Venice Saved* should reproduce this movement.)

*

There is a divine label on the social: an intoxicating mixture that encloses all licence. The devil in disguise.

And yet a city … (Venice …). But this is not what is social; it is a human milieu of which we are no more conscious than the air we breathe. A contact with nature, the past, tradition, a μεταξύ. [6]

Act Two. Violetta must appear when Jaffier's exultation is at its height. Once she is gone, Pierre makes a long speech in reply to Jaffier, who is silent; and when he says farewell to Pierre, he speaks as if under duress: 'You are right. What is a man or a woman at this moment, in comparison with us … ?'

Mix the Old Testament with Pierre's words.

Throughout the whole second act, Jaffier's words – to Pierre, to Renaud, to Violetta – are *all* ambiguous.

And what goes on in his soul remains mysterious.

Jaffier has only two moments of expansion in the second act. One is with Pierre, when he gives expression to friendship. The other is with Violetta, when he gives expression to love for Venice (made incarnate for him by Violetta – he tells her this later in a line, without the link being made clear). But even this expansion is contained. Contrast with the rush of words in the third act.

In the first act, a single rhythm – the zeal of the conspiracy.

In the second act, two – this zeal and Jaffier's immobility.

In the third, immobility.

*

The moment of Jaffier's meditation at the end of the second act is the moment when reality enters into him, because he has paid attention.

Pulsation in these two acts, giving a rhythm to time.

Theatrical pulsation.

Theatre (or epic). Third dimension in the order of human destiny. – *Oedipus Rex.* – *Bacchae.* – Jaffier … . [7]

Art and third dimension. And music?

*

Act Two. Make it clear that Jaffier's change of heart is supernatural.

Jaffier. It is supernatural to stop time.

It is then that eternity enters into time.

To believe in the reality of the external world and to love it: one and the same thing.

Ultimately, the organ of belief is supernatural love, even with respect to things below.

As soon as Jaffier realizes that Venice *exists* … .

*

The curse is transmitted. Indicate why Renaud, Pierre, Jaffier each became a man of adventure. (Same with the mercenaries and the courtesan.) Why (on a national scale) there exists this Spanish enterprise.

From the automatic transmission of evil to redemptive suffering.

*

Pity is an attribute that is truly divine. There is no human pity. Pity implies an infinite distance. There is no compassion for what is near. Jaffier.

*

Happy innocence. Violetta. Something that is also infinitely precious. But it is a precarious happiness, fragile – a happiness of chance. Apple blossom. This happiness is not linked to innocence.

*

The furious zeal of the first two acts is still present in the condemned men at the start of the third, violently constrained by chains and imminent execution, and torture. It must be visible.

Only Jaffier has not been carried away by this zeal, even for a moment. He is immobile at all times, as are Violetta and her father. All the others are violently carried away.

Zeal and intense dynamism in this play until Jaffier's monologue. There, zeal stops dead. The rest is only the stamping of feet.

The third act is composed of two parts. Jaffier speaks and nobody replies. People speak to him and he does not reply.

Even in the scene of the condemned men: cries and no reply.

*

In Jaffier's supplication and despair: insist perhaps even more on the *silence* that answers him.

Afterwards, insist on Jaffier's silence.

*

Scene with those condemned to death. First part: very short. Second part goes on indefinitely. One of them: 'Let them kill me if they want to, but I do not want to be tortured.'

*

In this scene, the ordeal of the tortured and hanged mercenaries is mentioned.

'But it's not possible for *us* to be treated this way. We are gentlemen.' 'Ah, but they said it would happen.'

One officer: 'I am a gentleman and I do not want to be hanged.'

Another: 'I do not want to be tortured.'

Another: 'I want to be pardoned.'

*

The power of simple repetition, as found in Spirituals. [8] Repetition until your nerves begin to suffer. This is to be used in *Venice*. In the scene of those condemned to death. And in the insults to Jaffier.

*

In the third act, the Secretary only addresses Jaffier twice. Or even once? Only have him speak to the servant for the rest of the time? Yes.

Jaffier. Have him ask himself: 'Do I exist?' But above all: 'Have I been transformed into an animal?'

*

Scene where Jaffier is mute. There must be dramatic interest. And this interest must be: making him speak. 'Tell us why you betrayed first Venice and then your friends.' – 'What does a traitor think about in the act of treachery? Explain that to us. Tell us if you think you're as good at treachery as Judas was. Perhaps you haven't told us everything yet. Perhaps there are still one or two little secrets you haven't revealed. What if we tortured him a little here, while his friends are being tortured over there? Why should they have to suffer, while he remains unharmed?'

*

In the scene of those condemned to death, a brief dialogue; draw out the part where each man is given a monologue about his fate.

When the apprentice torments Jaffier, have him joined by another, to draw out the scene.

When Violetta arrives, everybody leaves. Violetta remains alone.

So the artisans' lines are omitted – or, better, are reported in the middle of the previous scene. At the beginning, perhaps, before the apprentice begins.

*

In the third act, instead of replies ('Where's that?' 'Thank you, I shall go have something to eat and drink.'), silence should be kept and the others should comment on his gestures (seizing the gold avidly). 'We don't need to ask why he betrayed his friends!'

Draw out a bit more this part of the act when he stays silent? Let his words, followed by those of Violetta, put an end to an intolerable tension.

*

At the end: 'It looks like he's going to speak.' – 'Well, well! So he does know how to speak! I thought he was mute!' – 'No, look, he's not saying anything.' – 'Oh yes he is, just listen.' And before that, the apprentice. Insist on this more. 'His silence angers me.'

*

To recapture, for the first time since Greece, the tradition of tragedy in which the hero is perfect.

*

Theatre. Theatre must manifest both interior and exterior necessity.

On the stage – the slow maturation of a deed, with the universe around it – then the deed is hurled into the world.

*

The verses. They won't 'sound right' unless they create a new time for the reader. And as with music (Valéry) a poem emerges from silence, returns to silence. [9]

Elements of the poem. A time that has a beginning and an end. To what does this correspond? Then the *flavour* of words: each word should have a maximal flavour between the sense ascribed to it and all its other senses; an agreement or an opposition with the sound of its syllables; agreements and oppositions with words before and after.

*

Venice Saved. Note. – The Marquis of Bedmar, Spanish ambassador to Venice, conceived a plan in 1618 to deliver Venice into the power of the Spanish King, who was at that time master of almost all of Italy, by means of a conspiracy. Desiring to stay in the shadows because of his position as ambassador, he entrusted the plan's execution to Renaud, an elderly French lord, and to Pierre, a Provençal pirate and a captain and sailor of repute. Renaud was in charge of the preparation, and Pierre of the military operations. They were able to win over a large part of the mercenaries in the Venetian garrison, together with many of the officers serving Venice, most of them foreigners. The plan was to take Venice by surprise in the middle of the night, simultaneously occupying the city's strategic points, while lighting many fires in every part of the city, in order to spread confusion. Anybody who resisted was to be killed. The chosen night was that before Pentecost. Jaffier foiled the plot, of which he was one of the leaders, by revealing it to the Council of Ten, out of pity for Venice. Historians, especially Spanish ones, have denied the authenticity of this plot, but their arguments are very weak. It is, however, absolutely certain that the Council of Ten had several hundred men executed and that Bedmar had to leave Venice.

Venice Saved

Subject: *The Spanish plot against Venice of 1618, as told by the Abbé de Saint-Réal.* [10]

Characters

> **JAFFIER**, *naval captain, Provençal*
> **PIERRE**, *the same*
> **RENAUD**, *Spanish lord*
> **THREE OFFICERS**
> **THREE MERCENARIES** *(nationality?)*
> **COURTESAN**, *Greek, Venetian subject*
> **SECRETARY OF THE COUNCIL OF TEN**
> **VIOLETTA**, *his daughter*
> **BASSIO**, *his favourite servant*
> *One of his servants*
> *An artisan (Venetian)*
> *An apprentice (Venetian)*

Place: *Venice. Act One: At the courtesan's house (close to Saint Mark's Square). Act Two: Saint Mark's Square (on the campanile?). Act Three: Saint Mark's Square, or rather the* Piazzetta.

Time: Act One: Very early in the day (long before dawn), the vigil of Pentecost (Festival of Venice's Marriage to the Adriatic). [11] *Act Two: same day. Act Three: The day of the festival, starting in the middle of the night and finishing at daybreak. (In all, a little more than twenty-four hours.)*

Act One

Scene One

First part: Before Renaud's speech. (NB All the characters are assumed to be there for the whole act, moving around in the room.)

TWO OFFICERS

In a few hours we shall see day rise for the last time on this great city of Venice. Tomorrow's dawn will rise on a possession of the King of Spain and nothing more, and *we* shall be the ones responsible, a pack of exiles and so on.

They recall the ordeals and the arbitrary acts that have turned most of the conspirators to adventurers – insist on this.

Words about the conspiracy, about the prospects of glory and fortune, about the Marquis of Bedmar (Spanish Ambassador to Venice), Renaud, Pierre, Jaffier. Each is praised (quick portrait), but Jaffier most of all. They would like to have him as their leader. He is a born leader; haughty, very proud, but at the same time just and almost tender. He was born for great things. It is he rather than Pierre who ought to … . But he is happy for Pierre; they are such friends! Moreover, there is a marvellous unity among the conspirators; it is truly a band of chosen men. The secret is guarded in absolute security. Various words; projects for the future.

Scene Two

OFFICER, PIERRE, then JAFFIER, RENAUD. OTHER OFFICERS

The officer congratulates Pierre on the greatness awaiting him. The coming night he will lead the execution of the project: the capture of Venice. Afterwards he will be Governor of Venice and its dependent territories, in the name of the King of Spain. It is effectively over; their success is certain. What glory and what power! But this

is what you deserve. He asks for his favour as he attains power.
Pierre promises it, recognizing that he is a happy man, but among
all the favours that he has been granted by fortune, there is one
in comparison with which the others are nothing in his eyes: that
he has a friend. Conversation about this friend, this friendship,
friendship in general.

PIERRE

Jaffier is much more deserving than I am of such a great fortune.
But the thought does not occur to him; he is happy that I have been
granted it. While I should be happy to give it away to him. What
could ever separate two friends who are not separated by ambition?

OFFICER

They say that the best friendships can be broken by a woman.

PIERRE

This would never happen with us. For me, you see, one young and
pretty woman is no better than the next, and there are plenty of them.
All I ask of them is pleasure. I should not hesitate a second before
sacrificing some mistress of mine for my friend. And Jaffier is one
of those men who, when they love a woman, respect her to the extent
that they will also respect her choice, even if she loves another man.
And I think that if he loved a woman to whom he thought I was
attached, he would never admit this love, not even to himself *(insist*
on this). Anyway, we have often told each other that we have never
experienced a love that has come anywhere near our friendship.
I alone am close to him, and he to me. You cannot imagine what
this friendship of ours is like. Nothing could ever endanger our
friendship. Every man here is like a brother to me, and Jaffier feels
the same, but the two of us are much more than brothers. I should
take no pleasure in this present good fortune if I were not able to
share the joy with him.

OFFICER

Renaud is going to speak.

RENAUD

Long speech, given with great enthusiasm, detailing all the facts of the conspiracy. The goal is depicted with fervour.

In this speech, constantly *refers to the previous biography of the conspirators as a sub-plot. Almost all of them are adventurers, thrown into this way of life by distress and violence. Renaud, an exile from France, Pierre and Jaffier from Provence and so on.*

You are going to make history. You will destroy a power that is tyrannical, full of intrigue, hated by its own citizens and which opposes the unity of Europe. Thanks to you, the whole of Europe will be united under the Habsburg dynasty, and the ships of this united Europe will cross the seas to conquer the entire globe, bringing civilization and Christianity, as Spain has done for America. And all that will be thanks to you. [12]

Including this:

If peace is not imposed on Europe by Habsburg domination, the continent may be ravaged by thirty years of war. The House of Austria is close to universal domination; if it allows it to slip away, then Europe will be engulfed in long and ruinous bloody battles.

Turkish danger. Necessity of a united Christendom etc. Make it seem as if Spain has been pushed into such an enterprise by exterior *necessity. This theme of being driven by necessity – both on the individual and on the national level – is most obvious here, and, in the second act, in the encounter between Renaud and Jaffier.*

And so, even though our plan's execution is of necessity going to be terrible,

Description of the sack of the city, in six or seven lines – or more?

do not let that stop you. It is a temporary evil for a lasting good.

Evoke the Old Testament. [13]

Your glory and so on.

As adventurers, their ambition can only be fulfilled in such enterprises.

In all this first part: joy, pride, intoxication in action and in power without any shadow of concern. Rajas. [14]

Scene Three

RENAUD, PIERRE

Second part: after the speech.

Pierre congratulates Renaud after his speech. He notes that he is concerned, wonders why? Everything is going well, after all. Renaud, despite finding this difficult to say, explains that while he was speaking he saw Jaffier's face go pale and lose its composure as Jaffier listened. Such weakness makes him fear for everything. He fears losing everything and, to stop this happening, proposes having Jaffier killed. Pierre's horror, protests; he vouches for Jaffier. He knows his valour, his faithfulness, his tenderness for his friends. Jaffier entered the conspiracy out of friendship for Pierre (remind how). He entered, took an oath – out of pure affection for Pierre, without even knowing what the conspiracy was about, when he was far from Venice. Pierre summoned him for the conspiracy (?). And he would betray such friendship? Why? Out of fear? Jaffier has never been afraid. He has always been valiant, impetuous, reckless when it comes to defending those he loves ... Renaud insists. He has great experience, he is acquainted with this sort of man, the sort who gets involved in great enterprises but loses his nerve at the moment of execution. It was precisely at the moment when Renaud was describing the execution that Jaffier's face changed. His courage for this conspiracy cannot be deduced from the acts of courage he has shown in the past. A conspiracy demands a particular type of courage, and even a man who is prepared to confront many other perils may lack the heart for it. In such a case, the only remedy is death. Certainly this is sad; Renaud loves Jaffier, too, but it is necessary. What is one human life when you are about to change the world? Pierre tries to show that Jaffier cannot be killed, from the point of view of the conspiracy. He is so loved, admired and respected that he cannot disappear without consequences. It will make no difference whether Renaud gives the true explanation to the conspirators or not: the trouble will be great. Pierre calls an officer.

Scene Four

RENAUD, PIERRE, OFFICER

PIERRE, *to the officer*

We wonder, Renaud and I, who would be the right man to replace me if anything happened to me.

OFFICER

Jaffier, of course. Everybody would give you the same answer.

PIERRE

And what do you think of Jaffier? I am so close to him that I sometimes wonder what he seems like to those who know him less well.

Brief praise of Jaffier by the officer. Natural leader. They want to obey him. Dignity, justice. Pierre dismisses him and calls the other.

Scene Five

RENAUD, PIERRE, OTHER OFFICER

Same scene effectively. The praise of Jaffier is quite different (companion of Jaffier when they were imprisoned by the Moors, and then escaped? Depict his constancy under the blows of fate, and his serenity, which could at times be troubled by pity?).

Scene Six

RENAUD, PIERRE

PIERRE

You see. You cannot just have him disappear without creating serious unrest among the men.

RENAUD

I do realize that, but I still think that if he were to pose a serious threat to us, then his death would be the only solution.

PIERRE

So you would say that to *me*, when I would give up for him the throne of Germany if it were offered to me at that price? You know that I would sacrifice the whole world and every man alive for him? You think that his life poses a danger to you, but if I were to become your mortal enemy, ready to do whatever it took to bring you down … don't you think that might also be dangerous?

RENAUD

Do not talk like this; I shall do nothing without your consent. When I engaged you for such a great enterprise, one that will change the face of the earth and decide the fate of centuries to come, I thought that you would be committed to sacrificing every sentiment to our enterprise. We demanded such resolution from each man.

PIERRE

Yes, every sentiment. That's true. Apart from one. Apart from my friendship. Ask me anything else, but leave my friend alone.

RENAUD

Very well, I yield, and I hope your confidence in him is not misplaced. But listen carefully; I feel that your friend could lose us. He had a moment of weakness, and will have others. You will regret not having listened to reason. To be a good conspirator, you should love nothing.

PIERRE

I know him. He will be our greatest support, you'll see.

RENAUD

I only hope you are right, but I fear the contrary. No matter, let us go sleep for a few hours.

Scene Seven

A final scene, short, where one of the officers says:

OFFICER

Look, dawn is starting to break. By the next dawn, this city will lie prostrate at our feet and we shall be the masters.

Curtain

Act Two

Scene One

PIERRE, RENAUD

Pierre has been ordered by the Council of Ten to appear before them immediately. He does not see this as a bad sign, but cannot disobey without exciting suspicions. But he has a good idea: Jaffier will replace him this night. He will command the conspirators' capture of the city and then will be in charge of commanding Venice and its dependant territories. Thus, even if there has been a moment of weakness – which Pierre does not believe – this responsibility and power will restore Jaffier's courage. Pierre is happy to think that he will have the good fortune he deserves. Pierre has already had this substitution accepted by the Marquis of Bedmar, on condition that Renaud agrees. Renaud consents, but is astonished.

RENAUD

I for one would not give up for anything the reward that I've been promised for my part in the conspiracy: you know that I am to have a high responsibility at the Court of Madrid.

He is convinced that thinking beings tend without exception to exercise all the power it is possible for them to exercise. This seems to him to be the law of thinking beings, just as gravity is the law of matter. [15] To give up power voluntarily seems to him to be against nature.

PIERRE

That's because you have no idea what friendship is. You would be right if this were anybody other than Jaffier. But Jaffier is more me that I am myself. Here he is. Would you leave us for a while? I shall sound him out.

Scene Two

PIERRE, JAFFIER

Pierre announces to Jaffier his new office, almost drily. Jaffier: explosion of simultaneous regret and gratitude.

JAFFIER

You are the only man in the world capable of this. But I do not want it. I shall replace you tonight, but afterwards … .

PIERRE

No, no, it is better like this. This great fortune is by rights more yours than mine. You are by far the more capable man. At last you will possess the city you love – and how you love this city! You will be its master.

JAFFIER

Yes, all this beauty will be mine; how can I even imagine it?

In this evocation (which would be best given to Jaffier), mention should be made of the time (noon), the course of the sun and the light.

Friendship and happiness, crescendo; at the zenith, Violetta arrives.

Scene Three

PIERRE, JAFFIER, VIOLETTA

Violetta is bursting with joy because of the festival.

VIOLETTA

Oh! I wish it were tomorrow! Have you never seen the Festival of Venice? Nothing in this world is comparable; you shall see, tomorrow! What joy for me! Tomorrow I shall be able to show you my city in its most perfect splendour! There will be such beautiful music ... .

(Monteverdi) etc. [16] *She regrets that Pierre cannot be there; at least Jaffier will see ... etc. Pierre and Violetta talk politely, but Jaffier speaks little.*

Scene Four

PIERRE, JAFFIER

JAFFIER

You seem to have a liking for this girl. Do you have any instructions for me, about what to do with her tonight? Should she be kept safe?

PIERRE

Absolutely not, you'd be lost if you worried about that sort of thing when the time comes. There'll be too many important things to keep an eye on. It's true that she pleases me. After our victory I shall take her with pleasure, if she hasn't been killed or ruined during the sack. In any case, I shall have plenty of others. From tomorrow, we shall be able to take our pick of the noble girls; especially you, so handsome and noble and the future master. But enough of this. Listen: you know all the measures that have to be taken tonight, don't you?

JAFFIER

Yes.

PIERRE

And – forgive me for asking this question, I know the answer but my duty makes me ask it – you are ready to assume the command of an enterprise as glorious as this one, aren't you? You feel no fear, no concern as action gets closer?

JAFFIER

I'm certainly not afraid; what is there to be afraid about when an enterprise has been prepared as well as this one? I shall be happy to lead such a great action, to command men of such valour and unity that may not be seen again for centuries to come. So, no worry, no – except that, this night when Renaud was speaking, I couldn't help being a little disturbed, feeling pity at the idea of the city being sacked.

PIERRE

Ah! So that was what made you go pale! But that's nothing. Many great men have felt a moment of pity and have even shed tears just before bringing a great action to its end. But this never made them hesitate. The Romans wept for Carthage, but they destroyed it. [17]

Allusion to Cortés? [18]

The harm that we shall do is necessary. In any case, it will be brief and there will be little of it. Pity never stopped anybody. It's a superficial emotion. It often affects men with generous hearts, but never gets to the bottom of their soul. Those who say they were stopped in their tracks by pity are only using the word to disguise their fear. But you, my friend, you have never known fear, and what joy it is to think that we are going to cover ourselves in glory. I wish it were tomorrow. What a day that will be for us! What joy to know that tomorrow you will finally be in the state you deserve to be in, at the centre of everything and everyone.

Pierre describes their personal destinies and their miserable past.

JAFFIER

How could I not try to surpass myself on this coming night, so as to be worthy of a friend such as you? There is no part of me that is not set on the execution of our plan.

PIERRE

See, my friend, the glory that will be ours for a single night's effort! What fruit is within your grasp! You only have to pluck it.

The sweet fruition. [19]

See the city at your feet. This is how it will be tomorrow!

Perhaps:

PIERRE

My beloved friend, now you are ready for the victory.
This city is yours, and tonight you will take hold of it
in a mortal grasp that its body can only obey.
You will possess it. How wonderful to be the master!
You were born for this, to conquer, to be a commander.
Tomorrow, friend, tomorrow, how good it will be to meet,
and you will describe our triumph as we walk together
through this great city that shall be entirely our own!
Yours and mine, my friend. Ah! I wish that it were tomorrow.

*Change the order. Violetta is to arrive at the end of the dialogue
between Pierre and Jaffier, at the point where Jaffier's exaltation is
at its height, just after these lines. When she has gone, only the end
of the dialogue is about her. Jaffier says practically nothing, except
at the end:* 'You are right, what is a man or a woman compared with
an enterprise such as this?'

Here is Renaud. Follow carefully all his advice. This man possesses
a spirit of amazing acuteness. He is an inexhaustible treasure of high
political wisdom.

*Very short portrait of Renaud. (NB Has Jaffier slept between I and
II? Between II and III he does not sleep.)*

Scene Five

PIERRE, JAFFIER, RENAUD

PIERRE, *to Renaud*

I leave, and my mind is more at ease about the success of our
enterprise than if I were to stay. You can believe me; I know my

friend; none of us was made for great things the way he was. He is far superior to all of us, and he will show it. What happiness that he should be there to replace me! Otherwise, I should leave with great concern. I have never been afraid in my life, although I have encountered great perils, but I admit that if there is one thing that is capable of making me tremble, then that is the refined tortures of the Republic of Venice. Everyone agrees that even a hero would not be able to bear them. The very possibility of falling alive into the hands of the Council of Ten would make me shiver with fear, if there were any risk of that. But with my friend directing this night's enterprise, there is no danger. We have foreseen everything: his resolution, his bravery and his prudence are beyond compare. Success is inevitable. Give him the same instructions you gave me, Renaud. I shall see you soon, my friend; I am only leaving you for a day. Tomorrow, at this time, we shall be together, victorious and full of glory.

Scene Six

JAFFIER, RENAUD

This scene is a lesson in high politics given by Renaud to Jaffier, to prepare him for his new responsibilities. Renaud congratulates Jaffier in a tone of deep respect. Then some technical details. Jaffier asks him about what measures he proposes be taken to limit the damage during the sack of Venice.

RENAUD

Above all, put this concern out of your mind.

JAFFIER

But is it not my duty to make sure that this city is given to the King of Spain in the best possible condition?

RENAUD

This sense of duty does you honour, but you would lose everything, were you to have such a concern at this moment. That time will come, but only after our victory. Not even tomorrow. Let's say, the day after tomorrow.

Explanation. (The order of this explanation is not definitive.)

See this city and all those who dwell in it as a toy that can be thrown about, even broken. You must have realized that this is the feeling of your mercenaries, even of your officers. We, of course, are above that; we are making history. And yet, for me, when it comes to us … *(another reminder of the hard times that they have gone through and their condition as adventurers, as exiles)*, it is a delicious pleasure to see today these men of Venice, so proud, who think that they exist. They each believe they have a family, a house, goods, books, rare paintings. They take themselves seriously. And as of now they no longer exist. They are but shadows. Yes, that gives me pleasure, but for us the pleasure is incidental. For the soldiers, it's the only pleasure. What does history matter to them, at least to most of them? And tonight's enterprise will give them neither fortune nor glory; afterwards, they shall be soldiers as they were before. We have to give them this city for one night as their plaything. Even for the next day. Above all, you as leader – if you have any particular friends in Venice, then do not try to protect them. The officers would then want to do the same. This sort of compassion is fatal to an enterprise such as ours. It dampens the spirit of our troops. They must have full licence to kill anything that resists them. Even what pleased them. Only licence like this can give our action the necessary devastation that will bring victory.

But acting like this is also in the interest of the people of Venice themselves. These people who from tomorrow will be subjects of the King of Spain. We must destroy their courage once and for all, in their own interest, so that afterwards we can get them to obey without any bloodshed. There is no other way of reaching that goal. Because – despite what I said in my speech to the conspirators – almost all of them hate Spain and are passionately attached to their country and to their freedom, the people as much as the nobles. So, if you don't destroy their courage once and for all, sooner or later they will revolt, and putting down this revolt will cause more bloodshed and more damage to your reputation than all the horrors of the sack.

The cruelties of this night will do no harm to your reputation, for everybody knows the licence soldiers are allowed in a sack. You will stop this licence when it has gone far enough; as you are the one who restored order and security after the terror, the locals will obey you blindly. They will obey you in spite of themselves, but this is how a true leader likes to be obeyed. And they will love you almost at once, for they will expect both good things and bad things to come from you alone, and people love the one on whom they depend absolutely. But it is necessary for this night to have changed them. Look at them: proud, free and happy. Tomorrow, none of them must dare to raise their eyes before the least of your mercenaries. Afterwards, it will be easy for you to govern the city peacefully and with glory for yourself, as long as you are careful to humiliate the nobles, which will terrify the people. Then you must get the bourgeois on your side by giving them the offices that the nobles refused them; of course, these offices will now carry no authority. The nobles must now have no place in society. They were too proud to speak to strangers, and now they will only be able to trade, marry or travel if they are prepared to spend long hours in Spanish antechambers, waiting for permission.

Tonight and tomorrow these people must feel that they are mere toys. They must feel lost. Suddenly, and forever, the ground must vanish from beneath their feet. They will only find equilibrium by obeying you. So it does not matter how harshly you govern them. Even those who lost a father or a son to the soldiers under your command, or who saw a sister or a daughter dishonoured, will regard you as a god. They will cling to you the way a child clings to a mother's coat. But, for this to happen, nothing must be respected tonight. Everything they hold eternal and sacred, their bodies and the bodies of those they love, everything must be seen to be given as a toy to the big children known as soldiers. Tomorrow they must no longer know where they are. They must no longer recognize anything that surrounds them. They must no longer recognize themselves. And this is why, apart from those who resist (and who must all be killed, of course), it would be a good idea if the massacres went a stage further, so that some of the survivors will have been forced to have watched somebody they love being killed or dishonoured. Afterwards, they will do what we want.

JAFFIER

I see this city, so beautiful and powerful and peaceful, and I think that in one night we, a few unknown men, will become its masters. And I think I must be dreaming.

RENAUD

Yes, we are dreaming. Men of action and enterprise are dreamers; they prefer dream to reality. But they use arms to make others dream their dreams. The victor lives his dream; the vanquished lives another's dream. All the men of Venice who live through the next night and day will spend the rest of their lives wondering if they wake or dream. But, as of tomorrow, their city, their liberty and their power will seem to them to be more unreal than a dream. Arms make a dream stronger than reality; this is the stupor that brings about surrender. As of tomorrow, they must believe that they have always been subjects of Spain, that they have never been free. The sky, the sun, the sea and the stone monuments will no longer be real in their eyes. As for the children, they will be born without roots. But the shock must be violent enough to rob them forever of any feeling of what is real. It is good that the night of our enterprise should be the one preceding the festival, that the dawn that was to have been that of the festival should rise on their ruin. Excellent training. Tomorrow they shall get up for something very different from a festival.

Etc. Theme of unreality. Carthage, Cartagena, Persepolis. [20]

It will also be good for your rule to be harsh, once you have put an end to the troops' licence and re-established order and security. Their entire life must be changed – their daily life. They are to feel day by day that they are not at home, but in somebody else's home, and at the mercy of somebody else; this is the only way they will obey without bloodshed. Otherwise, how would they ever resign themselves to having lost everything in one night? It will be good if many churches and frescos are destroyed; in their place we shall build churches in the Spanish style. When they constantly see what they hate, even when they turn to God, they will realize that they were born to obey. It will be necessary to forbid completely all their songs, plays and festivals. Their painters and musicians will be sent to the Court of Madrid; they will be valued there. The local people must feel like strangers in their own home. This has always been and always will be the policy of conquerors: to uproot the conquered. We must kill this city to the point where the citizens feel that a revolt, even if it were successful, would not be able to bring it back to life; therefore they will submit. Your wishes, your fantasies, your dreams: you are now the master and from now on these must be the sole reality for them. You will be one of those men who force an entire people to live out his dream. When you even think of somebody's death, that person will die. Every object on every day will remind somebody – this is absolutely necessary – that he is alive only as long as you want him alive. And their life as well will model itself on your thought. Their life and their death will only be your dream. Is there a more glorious destiny? Such is the sweet fruition of victory! How happy you must feel!

Jaffier interrupts this exposition with frequent replies and questions. At the beginning his tone is one of respect, ardour and sincere admiration; then it gradually becomes more sombre, dry and cold. At the end he thanks Renaud in a dry and haughty voice, praises his wisdom, declares himself determined to follow his perfectly wise advice on all points; meanwhile he will finish the preparations.

Ambiguous words of Jaffier at the end:

JAFFIER

I am overwhelmed by the truth of your words, and shall conduct myself accordingly.

Jaffier shows himself (and is) totally convinced by the soundness of Renaud's arguments, which he understood from the first words. He goes.

Scene Seven

RENAUD *(alone)*

Pierre was right. This Jaffier was made for great things.

Praises also his high intelligence, which must have been hinted at by his replies.

I am only astonished that he does not seem more joyful about the great fortune awaiting him. But he is certainly incapable of fear. I must have seen it all wrong. I made an error. I don't know why I still feel worried, though.

Scene Eight

RENAUD, OFFICERS

The officers inform Renaud about difficulties they are having with the mercenaries, who cannot prevent themselves from treating the Venetians with insolence. This could excite suspicion. Then a few details about the conspiracy. Joy, intoxication in the game.

OFFICER I

We approach the crucial moment. ... Like in my childhood games
... .

Does one of them refer to Plutarch? [21] *(Cf. Retz.)* [22] *Description of the pleasure of sacking a city; memories.*

OFFICER II

All these proud bourgeois – and the sight of a sword will make them see right away that the soldier is master. And so, hoping to be well treated, they'll be respectful, submissive and as trusting as children. I've seen them clutching the cloak of a soldier who was beating them, during one sack ... .

Renaud takes no part in this dialogue.

Scene Nine

RENAUD, OFFICERS *(silent)*, MERCENARIES

Renaud reprimands the mercenaries.

RENAUD

No insolence today! You're going to lose everything! And do you know what awaits us if we're discovered before it begins? Tomorrow, you shall be as insolent as you wish. Tomorrow, all day, you will have complete freedom. You will enter into the homes of the bourgeois and the nobles and do what you want!

Perhaps:

RENAUD

See this city, so full of murmurs, lying at your feet.
All of it is for you to treat however you please.
You will kill at random, in play, as your fancy takes you,
And all the survivors will see light only at your whim.
Tomorrow and days that follow: all will give way to you.
The proudest citizens will lower their eyes as you pass.
None of them will dare oppose anything that you might wish.
    For today you must pretend.

The mercenaries make brief promises to obey. Renaud leaves.

Scene Ten

OFFICERS, COURTESAN, MERCENARIES *(silent)*

The courtesan asks the officers how things stand. She is impatient and exultant.

OFFICER I

You hate Venice that much?

She tells her story. The Venetian governor of the Greek island where she was born (to the noblest local family) seduced her after a formal promise of marriage. When her father tried to force him to keep his promise, he had him assassinated. She came to Venice to seek justice; instead of being granted it, she was ruined by the procedural costs. Finding herself alone in Venice and without resources, she had to

*become a courtesan. She has all the possible rancour towards Venice
of a woman of noble sentiment who has been reduced to such a level.*

OFFICER II

Do you really think you can get us to believe a story like that? Every
courtesan in Venice tells it, or else a very similar one. Why lie, to us
of all people?

COURTESAN

What? I am a *liar*?

She is about to leave in anger.

OFFICER I

Come on, don't get angry. Tonight we'll make you the Queen of
Venice. All your wishes shall come true. What do you wish for?

She replies with wild hatred for the families.

COURTESAN

All the men here who have insulted me: I have their names. I want
their wives and daughters to be given to the soldiers. And also the
wives and daughters of all those who helped govern this state. What
pleasure I shall have tomorrow when I see the survivors choking
with shame! I shall mock them and they will not dare reply!

In this scene, is there an allusion to the story of the six noble girls?
[23]

The officers leave with the courtesan, joking.

Scene Eleven

MERCENARIES

*Envious of the officers because of their relationship with the
courtesan. Console themselves by thinking about what is waiting for*

them that night and the next day. Describe the delights of sacking. Memories. Praise of Renaud.

ONE MERCENARY

He understands us, at least; he knows we need pleasures like this. Our troubles, our dangers … .

Pass over this lightly.

And when we can no longer serve because we are maimed or too old, we have to take to the road, with no roof over our head. If we want to eat, we must stretch out our hand. And with what insolence these bourgeois give their miserable alms … or more often refuse! Aren't we entitled to revenge from time to time?

Wish that the night would come soon. Glorious enterprise, without risks. Happiness of killing people surprised in their sleep.

ANOTHER

Perhaps not even one of us will be killed. It's hard to believe when you see them walking by in all their pride, but tonight, surprised as they sleep, they will be like sheep. They will have their throats cut like sheep, without defending themselves.

See Violetta and her father. Prefer not to meet them, and leave. But before this, exchange vulgar jokes about Violetta.

A MERCENARY

I shall ask to be responsible for killing him, and the girl is mine; I want to be the first.

ANOTHER MERCENARY

What are you talking about? That one is for the officers.

FIRST MERCENARY

No, she's not. The officers will have enough noble girls. This one isn't noble. She's just right for us. I want to be first. Or if some officer really wants her, then I'll be second. Afterwards you lot can do whatever you please; kill her if it amuses you.

Scene Twelve

VIOLETTA, THE SECRETARY OF THE COUNCIL *(her father)*

They speak of the next day, of the festival. Violetta expresses her happiness. She does not know why, but she feels happy, so happy, almost too happy. And tomorrow she will be still happier, for tomorrow is the festival. Everything is smiling on her, nothing can harm her, nothing can threaten her. One year ago she was still a child and was unable to rejoice as intensely as she will rejoice the next day. She does not know what transformation has been produced in her. She does not know what is going on. But the sky, the sea, the light, the gondolas, the people, everything she sees, everything she does – all this overwhelms her with happiness.

VIOLETTA

What a day tomorrow will be! How wonderful it will be to wake at dawn and to say: it's today!

THE SECRETARY

What is this, child? Might you be in love with somebody?

VIOLETTA

No, nobody. I don't know what it is; I feel I'm going to fall in love. I also feel I love the entire universe. How many good and lovely human beings there are, Father!

THE SECRETARY

I had been wondering if you weren't in love with Pierre, or Jaffier. I've seen you blushing when you look at them. It also seemed to me that they both have feelings for you, especially Jaffier. Even if they are foreigners, and even if their fortune is far from suitable for our family – I like them both so much that I should not object if you loved either of them.

VIOLETTA

Father, I always thought I could never love a foreigner. How would a foreigner ever understand me, not knowing the happiness of being born as a member of a city such as this? And yet it's true that these two men of Provence are valiant and courteous. Jaffier especially is handsome and generous and there's something about him that makes everyone love him. But, Father, look how beautiful Venice is today, in this light! Ah! She will be much more beautiful tomorrow.

In this scene, the Secretary speaks in prose and Violetta speaks in unrhymed or rhymed verse, depending on whether she is speaking to her father or to herself.

THE SECRETARY

Come on, now.

VIOLETTA

Father, haven't you got several hours to spend with me to celebrate our happiness? Affairs of state can't be that pressing.

THE SECRETARY

But, child, if we weren't there to look after the state's security, your beautiful Venice would soon be destroyed by the sword and by fire, or at least enslaved to the Spanish.

VIOLETTA

Oh! Father, how can you speak of such a thing! It doesn't even bear thinking about!

Jaffier and the officers enter at this moment; they hear the last two replies of the Secretary to Violetta.

Scene Thirteen

THE SECRETARY OF THE COUNCIL, VIOLETTA,
JAFFIER, OFFICERS *(silent)*

VIOLETTA, *to Jaffier*

Isn't it true that it's unthinkable that Venice could ever be destroyed
or enslaved? How would we live? We could not live. We should be
in a desert.

Cf. Renaud's words, Scene VI.

That will never, never happen. God would never permit the
destruction of something so beautiful. And who would to do
evil to Venice? The most despicable enemy would not have the
heart. What benefit would there be for a conqueror in suppressing
Venetian liberty? Only a few more subjects. Who would want –
for so little gain – to suppress something so beautiful and unique!
To do evil to Venice! Its beauty is a better defence than that of
soldiers, better than the concerns of statesmen! Isn't that true,
Signor Jaffier?

*All this is interrupted by Jaffier's replies. He agrees with Violetta,
his tone a mixture of light badinage and enthusiasm. Progressively,
from reply to reply (in couplets?), Jaffier's tone turns from badinage
to love for Venice. There must be a resonance of pain in everything
he says. This is one of the key points of the play.*

JAFFIER

No man could ever make something as beautiful as Venice. Only
God. The greatest thing a man can do, the thing that brings him
closest to God, is to preserve the marvels that exist, given that he
cannot create them.

*He, although a foreigner, would gladly give his life to preserve
Venice. Violetta is happy at these words. She is sorry that Jaffier is
not from Venice.*

THE SECRETARY, *to Violetta*

My child, who would have thought that a city would be defended by its beauty! And luckily we have more serious reasons to be reassured; thanks to our care and our good fortune, there is nothing that menaces us just now. But, child, you do realize that no city has ever been preserved through the pity of an enemy? In your games, haven't you ever plucked the leaves off a flower, broken a toy or pulled the wings off an insect?

VIOLETTA

Oh! No, never, never!

Then Violetta says to her father:

Tomorrow, at least, you need to have time for me. Why don't we spend a few hours in a gondola under the stars tomorrow evening, Father? Tomorrow evening, after an entire day of festivities. Not this evening, because I want to wake up tomorrow at dawn after a long sleep, for an entire day of joy. If you only knew, Signor Jaffier, what sort of day you are going to have tomorrow.

Violetta describes the festival. (This is perhaps where she should speak of Monteverdi.)

Jaffier replies and also speaks to her about what she will see and do on the next day. Violetta describes how the Venetians feel about the day of this festival.

Even after you've seen the festival, you won't know what it's like for a man or a woman of Venice. That is something that nobody can know.

THE SECRETARY

You see: here even our children share our feelings. And that shouldn't surprise you. The glory and the liberty of this city are more than 600 years old. Tomorrow isn't just a great day for the children, but for men as well. For me, this day will be a good one. Tomorrow you can ask me whatever favour you want, and I shall grant it.

Leaves with Violetta.

Scene Fourteen

JAFFIER, OFFICERS

The officers congratulate Jaffier on his recent stroke of good fortune and ask his favour, and his protection after the victory. (Perhaps some particular favours.) Praise his duplicity with the Secretary and Violetta. They could have sworn that he was sincere. Anyone who heard him might have thought that the festival was going to take place the next day.

OFFICER

I had to stop myself laughing when the Secretary promised him favours tomorrow! Tomorrow and the days after that – if by some miracle he is still alive – he'll be the one who keeps coming to each of us to ask for protection. Especially to you. After the King of Spain, you'll be our master and his.

Jaffier replies to none of this. The officers continue to speak. Speak of Violetta.

OFFICER III

One of my soldiers thinks he's going to be the first to have her.

OFFICER II

We go first, then the soldiers.

OFFICER I

It would be best if we forbade the soldiers to touch her; otherwise she'll be done for, and a girl like that could keep you happy for ages.

OFFICER II

Bah! There's no lack of pretty girls in Venice, and many of them are both beautiful and noble. Some will die tonight, but there'll still be plenty left.

Jaffier, brusquely starting to speak, drily gives various technical instructions for the capture of the city. The officers reply with respect.

JAFFIER, *to Officer II*

Sir, I know that several Venetian families receive you as a friend. If you want them to be kept safe, I shall be glad to make it happen.

OFFICER II

Oh no! It's true that I have been connected with several families, and they have been very useful to me during my stay here. I often told them that my sword was theirs in time of danger, and that was what I thought. Normally, I'd have risked my life for them without hesitation. But that's all in the past now! The decisive moment is at hand; all these people are like ants to me. Like shadows. They think they exist, but they are wrong. How can I spare them even a single thought when all my thoughts are fixed on the glory we are about to win?

JAFFIER

I was expecting this reply, and the only reason I asked was to test you.

OFFICER II

It's odd, but I don't think I can even remember who my friends here were. I once had the same thing happen to me when we sacked a town where I had some friends. I had forgotten that they existed. They saw me and threw themselves at me, clutching my cloak; I pushed them away, not even recognizing them.

Jaffier, in this scene, speaks very briefly (in one-line replies?).

Scene Fifteen

JAFFIER, OFFICERS *(silent)*, RENAUD

Renaud arrives, makes recommendations to Jaffier, a little verbosely but full of joy and excitement (he has finally put his worries to one side). Jaffier interrupts after a few lines, in the middle of a phrase, harshly and haughtily.

JAFFIER

I am the leader and know what I have to do. You, sirs, go there and there. You, sir *(to Renaud)*, see to these things (and come back and give me an account (?)).

Very dry orders. They obey without a word.

Scene Sixteen

JAFFIER *(alone)*

JAFFIER

The city and the people and the sea will be mine.
The peaceful city is in my hand and does not know;
but soon she will learn that she belongs only to me;
for now it draws near, the harsh moment when suddenly
my hand will grow firm and then destroy her.
Nothing can defend her. She is feeble and unarmed
and at my feet. And who is going to stop us now?
Slowly the sun will now sink down to the horizon;
when the last fires have flared on the sea and the canals,
the city will disappear forever.
Tomorrow's sun will not bring her back to see the day;
all that the breaking dawn will most cruelly reveal
is the corpse of a city where iron has passed through.
What iron has killed cannot be brought back by the sun.
Just a few hours more, and the city will be dead.
Some stones, a desert, scattered bodies that do not move.
Those who have survived will have become corpses themselves.
Astonished and mute, all that they will do is obey.
Having seen their loved ones either defiled or else killed,
they will hasten to obey the very men they hate.

Empty eyes will look around in vain
for palaces, houses or churches.
Their songs will never again be heard.
They will have no voice for their lament.
This sea for them will be always mute.
Day after day and for all their life
they will hear nothing, only orders.

It is through me, on this night, that terror, shame and death
will descend on them, and they shall have me for master.
Tomorrow, all those here will reluctantly obey.
Tonight the city is still happy in its splendour;
for yet one more evening her people are safe and proud.
The dying sun still covers her with its final rays.
If only it knew, then it would stop out of pity.
But the sun has no pity for her, nor, alas, do I.
Am I permitted to be as insensible as the sun,
a man whose eyes have seen the city that must perish?

Scene Seventeen

RENAUD, JAFFIER

Renaud returns, speaks of a small difficulty that had not been foreseen, an organizational detail. Praises Jaffier for the arrangements he has made and for the zeal that he has inspired in them all. Congratulates himself that Jaffier is in charge. No other man is so suited for extraordinary action.

In the first lines, he asks Jaffier a question. Jaffier does not reply. Renaud (not daring to comment on this) continues at some length. Jaffier completely silent. At last Renaud breaks off.

RENAUD

What is it? You're looking at me but don't seem to be hearing me. Is something wrong? Something troubling you?

JAFFIER

No, quite the opposite. I see clearly what I have to do. I am sure of success and perfectly resolute. I know that my companions and above all my friend have put their safety in my hands with complete trust. They were right to do so; neither death nor torture could make me weaken when I am responsible for the safety of men of such valour. I am resolved to do what I have decided to do to protect them from all danger. Nothing can make my resolution waver. Sir, leave now … . As for me, I shall go … . This day is coming to an end. Let's make sure we do the best with what remains of it.

The two poles of this act are the scenes between Renaud and Jaffier, and between Violetta and Jaffier (and the monologue). The rest can be written very quickly.

Curtain

This act, like the preceding one, is written for the most part in unrhymed verse of fourteen syllables. The Mercenaries speak in prose; Violetta in unrhymed verse of eleven syllables (5-6); Jaffier replies in unrhymed verse of thirteen syllables (5-4-4). Or in eleven as well? Or Violetta in thirteen? Or twelve (4-4-4)? Other exceptions?

Violetta's lines and Jaffier's when he replies to Violetta are in rhyme, but very weak rhyme (verging on assonance?) and in groups of four, five or six.

Act Three

Scene One

THE SECRETARY OF THE COUNCIL, BASSIO
(his favourite servant)

The Secretary recounts what happened on the evening of the previous day. Jaffier came to tell him that he had various urgent revelations to make to the Council of Ten concerning the security of Venice, but he would only do this if the Ten would guarantee under oath the safety of twenty persons of his choice.

(Do the very first words of the scene tell the audience that the city is saved?)

Without this oath, neither the threat of death nor any torture would ever be able to drag a word out of him. The Secretary saw at once that this was true, that neither terror nor even the refined tortures practised by Venice would be able to shake a man as resolved as Jaffier. He informed the Ten, who, despite their extreme reluctance to swear any such oath, authorized him to make a favourable reply. He brought Jaffier to them; seeing him, they had the same impression as the Secretary. They swore an oath, agreeing to his demand. He then revealed to them all the details of a conspiracy that was to be put into action that very night to put Venice under Spanish domination, taking it by surprise. Soon afterwards, the exactitude of the details was verified; without Jaffier, the enterprise would have been bound to succeed; the Secretary was still shuddering at the thought. When questioned about his motives in revealing the plot, Jaffier said that it was pity; when asked what reward he desired, he said that all he wanted was that the oath be respected. The twenty men whom he saved were the leaders and the principal conspirators. The Ten quickly had all the conspirators arrested. After a long deliberation, it became apparent to the Ten that the good of the state did not allow them to observe the oath sworn to Jaffier. Most of the conspirators, and almost all the mercenaries, are already dead; the most important men, including the ones Jaffier was trying to protect, are now in chains and any moment now will be taken to prison, where they will undergo first torture and then execution. Violetta knows nothing. She is sleeping and, fortunately, will doubtlessly only wake up when all this is over. He knows that her wish is to come to the see the sea and greet the day as soon as she wakes, and hopes that she will not notice that anything is wrong. He wants her to learn nothing, at least on this day: otherwise the festival she has been awaiting with such joy would be darkened for her, and her joy would be gone.

(Brief, but properly depicted.)

The Secretary is troubled about Jaffier. The Ten have charged the Secretary, if Jaffier shows himself willing to accept calmly the breach of promise, to offer him an important post in Venice's service. But the Secretary, knowing Jaffier's generous and impetuous nature, has no hope of this happening. In that case, the Secretary is to calm him down and make him leave Venetian territory, forcing him to accept gold and forbidding him to come back to this territory on pain of death. The Secretary hopes that Jaffier will only learn the truth after his friends are dead. Otherwise he is resolved to treat him with extreme brutality (in his own interest), even though he admires him, loves him, feels sorry for him and is in his debt. For Jaffier, once he learns that word has been broken, will be led by his generous nature to take an attitude that will make it necessary to kill him. This is something the Secretary wants to avoid, out of gratitude and friendship. In his own interest, the only way is to break Jaffier's courage at once, and for a long time, by treating him with brutality.

(He repeats here almost word for word Renaud's words about how Venice is to be treated in Act Two Scene Six.)

Replying to a question from Bassio, the Secretary says:

THE SECRETARY

At first he will explode with anger; be on your guard then, and use two of your men. Disarm him before he can draw his sword. When he sees that his anger is useless, his pain will erupt. When his laments are over, he will be silent; then he will try to persuade me. He will waste what little strength he still has. Then he will fall into a long depression. In this state, it will be easy to lead him out of Venice. In spite of his great courage, his impetuosity, his pride – I am not worried, because there is no man, no matter how strong, proud or impetuous, who cannot be tamed when he has been made to feel powerless.

Bassio, who interrupts his master's explanation with frequent questions and replies, cannot understand his feelings for Jaffier. In his eyes the conspirators are terrible criminals, bandits, and Jaffier is a thousand times worse because in addition he has betrayed his accomplices, his own friends. The Secretary and Bassio, noticing Jaffier, leave.

(This scene is in prose.)

Scene Two

JAFFIER *(alone)*

Short monologue in unrhymed verse of fourteen syllables. He has not slept. He has confidence in the word of the Ten, but does not understand the anxiety that makes him hang around outside the state prison. What will Pierre say about what he has done? Jaffier has robbed him and the others of glory and fortune … . Suddenly he notices men being led along in chains; he hides, but so that he can see and hear them.

Scene Three

PIERRE, RENAUD, THE THREE OFFICERS *(all in chains),*

GUARDS *(silent)*, JAFFIER *(hidden and silent)*

Scene in unrhymed verse of fourteen syllables. The guards stop the conspirators by the prison. Chained, they await imminent torture and death; their words run into one another.

OFFICER I, *explosion of cowardice*

They have to pardon me. I am not guilty. It wasn't me. I was forced.

Officer III: furious with Jaffier (after hearing what Renaud says).

Officer II: sang-froid of the man who has played well and lost. Reproaches the others for their attitude.

Renaud, stripped of his reason of state, naked. Horrible bitterness: not at dying, but at losing all hope of power, fortune and glory. He reveals his ambitions; the success of this affair was to have procured him a high position at the Spanish court, and he was hoping that his ability would allow him, little by little, to become the King's favourite, so that one day he would rule over all those territories owing allegiance to the Spanish crown – and even many others – in the name of the King. Bitter envy of Bedmar, who has failed but who will live and be able to succeed later. The dream that Bedmar carries in his heart continues. Bedmar will one day be able to impose his dream on men and on things. For him, however, the failure is final. Curses Jaffier, on whom he blames his loss. Curses himself for not having him put to death when the thought occurred to him. Curses Pierre for stopping him having Jaffier put to death.

Pierre is still sure about Jaffier. Sure that he is already dead, or, like them, in chains and awaiting death somewhere.

PIERRE

… For if he was alive and free, he would be close to us, fighting for us, even if he were alone, even if there were no hope!

(Insist on this.)

Pierre calls Jaffier.

Since we have to perish like this, if only at least we could be together!

Reproaches himself bitterly for being the cause of Jaffier's affliction, of Jaffier's death, because he forced him into the conspiracy.

(Insist on this.)

You trusted me. You followed me. And I led you to this loss. To death.

(To these tortures?)

Two parts to this scene. In the first and longer part (which begins with various mutual exhortations to remain brave, in a firm tone), the chained conspirators are conscious of existence, of the presence of the other men; they speak more or less for the benefit of the others; they talk among themselves. The end of this scene is the moment when, on account of Jaffier, Renaud and Pierre insult and accuse each other; there is a very brief passage (two lines, perhaps one each) where first Renaud addresses Pierre, then Pierre addresses Renaud, then officer I addresses both of them (in this order); like Plautus's slaves they evoke with joy the tortures that await them all. [24]

The second part finishes with the sudden arrival of the Secretary of the Ten; after which the conspirators process out in complete silence; when they have all left, Jaffier shows himself.

The second part of the scene is perhaps:

RENAUD

Who are they, who are they who have stolen my destiny?
That part in which I have a right to power and glory?
My intelligence raised me up on high like an eagle,
and, seeing the flock of those who were created to serve,
I conceived how I could dominate peoples from afar;
I thought I could be the favourite of the King of Spain,
make myself in his name the master of all Christendom;
conquer the Orient and command all of the known world;
do I have to die here? For then I shall never have lived.
I have never lived, because I have never yet governed.
No, this is not possible, you must live before you die.
They will kill me there, in prison, before the break of day;
and so I shall not reign; no, I shall never, ever reign!

OFFICER I

I shall inform on the others, and I shall be reprieved.
They can all perish, as long as I receive a pardon.

OFFICER II

Why do we stay here? How slow they are! Let there be an end!
Ah, let them make haste, for I weary of waiting for death.

RENAUD

I would have known how to rule a state as big as the world.
I was born for this. All my soul has been thirsting for it.
I did not possess my destiny even for a day.
I dreamed of so much, and I shall have accomplished nothing.
My dream is now over, for they are coming to kill me.
In my heart I bore, in secret, the empire of the world;
all that remains in me is nothingness; I am nothing.
There, in this prison, before daybreak, in just one moment,
the hangman's two hands will become my entire universe.
Why, why should this be? I can do no more. I am frozen.
Everything I wanted is about to fade forever.

PIERRE

If he were with me, I should be strong enough to bear it.
I cannot cope with not seeing my friend a final time.
My eyes, deprived of him, have no place where they can find rest.
My God, if only all of a sudden his voice were there,
if I could touch his hand, or could feel him looking at me!
How shall I leave life without seeing him a final time?
I desire him in vain; he is nowhere; all is empty.
This is how sudden death will seize the dissatisfied soul.
No, I cannot go to my death separated from him,
alone in the hangman's hands and alone in death's anguish.

RENAUD

If I could have only possessed for the space of a day ... .

Enter the Secretary of the Ten, accompanied by Bassio and several servants.

THE SECRETARY

Guards, take the criminals to prison.

Exeunt conspirators.

Jaffier appears.

Scene Four

JAFFIER, THE SECRETARY OF THE TEN, BASSIO,
SERVANTS *(armed)*

JAFFIER

Sir, explain to me the spectacle I have just seen.
The Ten will not have broken their oath, I am certain.

THE SECRETARY

Sir. Their Lordships, after a night of deliberation, have decided to
put all these criminals to death. No one can accuse them of not
keeping their word; everybody in Venice and abroad knows their
extreme scrupulousness when it comes to keeping their promises.
Reasons of state have forced them to take this step. It would be an
act of ingratitude to Providence, which has chosen to save the city by
the very means of one of those who conspired to bring it down – by
means of *you*, sir – if we were now to fail to take every precaution.
The criminals cannot stay alive if Venice is to be safe. As for you, sir,
their Lordships have been gracious enough to spare your life. The
Ten have even authorized me to give you gold, in recognition of the
service you have done. But you must leave Venetian territory and
never return, under pain of death. I have nothing else to say to you
and shall add not another word.

JAFFIER

Was it then only for this that I saved these wretched men?
Yesterday they were all lost: for them, death and slavery;

for me, glory and fortune; and we were sure of success.
I renounced everything, through pity, to keep these men safe,
and *you* are telling me – words that I still cannot believe –
you *dare* to inform me that my companions will be killed?
My friend is going to die, my one friend, all that I love?
Assassin, liar, coward! And you look into my face,
the face of your benefactor, whose pity has saved you.
Ah! You have deceived me! How cowardly they told their lies.
It is not finished! I shall punish those ungrateful men,
starting with you. Be on your guard! For now blood is about to flow.
Ah! Their blood will flow, and flow in streams, beneath my sword's
    blade.

THE SECRETARY

Bassio, disarm him.

JAFFIER

You have disarmed me! Do you think that you have beaten me?
Coward, do you hope to reduce me to begging to you?
I shall not do it. Rather let there be death and torture
for my friends, for me, for all that's dear to me in the world,
yes, a thousand deaths, before I shall bow down before you.
Just wait! It will come soon, the moment of your punishment!
The city that I hate, where all is vile, cruel and low,
I shall see it crumble, despite its pride, in just one day.
My eyes shall watch the fire as it devours it bit by bit.
And some of you will see the defiling of what you love
as it bows down in shame at the whim of the conqueror;
the others, massacred, will die with curses on their lips.
Afflicted man! For I could have seen all of this tonight,
could have feasted my eyes by now on such a spectacle.
What made me lose my way? What made me spare these assassins?
What does it matter? I shall wait now. Soon I shall see it,
done by others or by me, several days hence, or today.
A just heaven will punish all those who despise their oath.
If Heaven does not act, I shall know how to punish them.
Henceforth my only goal will be the downfall of Venice.

As for you, how I rejoice that you should still be alive,
for everything you love will soon perish before your eyes.
And afterwards, *you* will perish, cursing both death and life.
You will die in misery, and I shall be comforted.

THE SECRETARY

Bassio, keep your men around him, with drawn swords; on no
account is he to leave the circle. I'm going to wait for him to calm
down; I don't think it will take long. Then I shall go and have the
criminals executed as soon as possible.

JAFFIER

O my friend! Where has my friend gone now?
Does he already writhe and suffer?
Crushed beneath the terrors of his death?
Do they make him scream under torture?
All of my companions are locked up,
in the hangman's hands, beyond my aid.
I cannot, no, I cannot bear it.
My friend, this was not what I wanted.
My friend, forgive me. You will perish
and I'll have killed you, and I'm alive.
His bones are going to crack in torture;
his knees will tremble in front of death.
I have lost him. I can do nothing.
I'm alone, disarmed, without support.

THE SECRETARY

You see, Bassio? He's not dangerous any longer.

JAFFIER

My friend, what are you doing right now?
You called me as you walked towards death.
Perhaps in this moment you call me.
You're surrounded by your enemies,
experts who have been schooled in torture,

whose eyes feast on their victims' weakness.
Do they take pleasure when you go pale,
when you scream in vain for some pity?
You sense the approach of bitter death
and I bring you no help, none at all.
Please do not curse me in your distress.
I should like, I should like to save you.
I have given them all of my power.
I am disarmed. I can do nothing.

THE SECRETARY

Bassio, you'll wait here for the signal confirming that the condemned
men have been executed. Then you will take this man to the border,
under escort. You are responsible for him. Don't forget that the Ten
have decided to leave him alive. But on no account are you to allow
him out of your hands until he's over the border, and you are not to
let him talk to anybody. You will present him with the gold that the
Ten have ordered me to give him. When you have seen him leave
Venetian territory, you are to return at once.

JAFFIER

Let me speak to you, then, before everything is finished.
If, in my suffering, I have said words that have caused offence,
I withdraw them. Forgive me. Listen to what I now ask.
I want to be taken to the Ten for one final time.
Do not refuse me. Be so good as to hear my reasons.
You know that yesterday, if I had not taken pity,
we would have accomplished our mission very easily:
then the power I had over you would have been total.
This power was mine – only pity made me renounce it.
I placed it in your hands and all I received in exchange,
alas, was your word. And therefore you must listen to me,
because the only recourse that I now have is your word,
and so at least you have to let me remind you of it.
You know full well how much my companions mean to me,
and my friend most of all. My honour is even dearer.

I cherish my friend in the way that you love your daughter.
For me, all of this means just what your city means to you.
I had promised nothing to Venice, and yet I saved it,
renouncing out of pity so much power and glory.
Ah! Do you not feel forced to render pity for pity,
to preserve what I love, given that this was your promise?
You would lose nothing, while I – I have lost so very much!
If you allow my beloved companions to stay alive,
then you would still be keeping your city and your power.
These wretched captives can no longer even threaten you.
They will take an oath never to do harm unto Venice.
They will keep their word. And they will obey you forever.
Will you not spare me? For as for me, if you kill them,
then I shall have reason to make vengeance my affair.
And I am alive, because I was the one who saved you.
You're in the wrong. Yesterday, when I came to search you out,
I did not demand an oath that I should be kept alive;
only my friends. If, then, you still feel obliged to punish
a mission directed against this, your beloved city,
ah, kill me, kill me alone, and leave all my friends alive.
I was the leader. It would be just to put me to death.
You will tell them, alas, that I had delivered them all,
that you are killing a traitor, and that your grace saved them,
and when they realize this, it will make them faithful to you.
Just think: a group of men as valiant and bold as these
is rarely seen. How gracious it would be to save their lives.
Save them. Kill me. If you do this, then you will keep your word,
and you will preserve your honour. For if you kill my friends,
the entire world will learn of it through me, mark it well:
just how Venice understands a promise's sanctity.
You can only gain by leaving them alive. You cannot lose.
The Ten will understand. Take me to them without delay.
After all that I have done, you cannot refuse me this.

THE SECRETARY

Have you understood my orders, Bassio? I shall hold you responsible
for having them carried out.

JAFFIER

You don't reply? You will not even give me a reply?
Ah, you cannot treat me like this, treat me with such disdain!
Speak to me! Speak to me! Every moment is a torture,
every single moment when my friend is made to suffer.
Then turn your eyes towards me! For you owe me a reply.
I must see the Ten. Are you going to take me to them?

THE SECRETARY

I have said everything I had to say. There is nothing more to add.

JAFFIER

Have pity on the man who is on the ground at your knees
and who held, yesterday, your destiny within his hands.
I was the man who saved you. And yesterday you listened;
can my voice in this moment not even escape my lips?
Alas, I am nothing, and it is all mute around me.
If such had been my wish, then now the entire city
would be holding its breath at the slightest word I might say;
and *you* would have me for a master. Ah! Who held me back?
I would have at my feet a people without faith or fire.
All would be begging for life, and I would have them all killed.
Afflicted man! What have I said? Ignore this, I beg you;
I am insane. Distress has made my reason fall apart.
Forgive me, for it is you who have made me fall so low.
You, to whom I conferred my honour, as if to a vault,
have made me, alas, into the assassin of my friends,
a traitor. And yet there was a time when I had honour.
I know that I have not always been the wretch that I am.
You alone can give me back my honour and I beg you,
you to whom my spirit rises as if you were my God,
you who could offer the gift of liberty to my friend.
Benefactor, look at me. I belong wholly to you,
Your slave forever. My soul and my days are ever yours.
What, you turn away from me? You dare to refuse me this?
But I have rights over you; remember, I have your word;
I am your saviour. No, no, I'm sorry. I irritate;

I shall not speak like this. I shall stop invoking my right
and rely on tears, the sole right of the afflicted man.
Do not go away, for there are still things I must tell you.
Alas! Alas! What to say? Where can I still find the words?
I have nothing but words, having given my power away.
Weaponless, I must not waver in my supplication.
Without doubt, words alone are what will penetrate your heart.
As soon as I fall silent, my defeat will become certain.
I can do no more. Have pity, and look down on my pain.

THE SECRETARY

Bassio, I am leaving. Keep watch over this man until the criminals
are dead, then take him away from Venice and give him the gold that
their Lordships have been good enough to award him.

JAFFIER

What! You're leaving! No, no, you cannot just leave me like this.
I still have not said all that I wanted to say to you.
I'll be able to turn your heart, if you stay a moment.
I'm sure of this. You leave! Ah, if you are inflexible,
if it must be that my friends are facing death in their cells –
let them at least perish without knowing of my treason!
At least be silent of the shame to which you have brought me!
I cry to him in vain. He has left me without a glance.
Do you dare to stop me walking where I choose, you servants?
Permit me to go and speak to your master once again.
You have disarmed me. I can do nothing else, except pray.
Be good, and let me go. Take pity on this, my prayer.
Ah, even the servants will not deign to give me a glance.
   Sky, brilliant sun upon the city,
   sea, canals, marble mixed with water,
   I speak to you and not to these men,
   because men will not listen to me.
   I was the one who saved your splendours.
   I, afflicted man, have lost my way.
   I perish for you; may you be cursed;
   may you perish also in your turn.

Once, men would listen to me. When I spoke, they would reply.
My word would carry what I wanted to the ears of men.
I myself was a man. And now I'm like an animal.
And in my greatest need my voice can no longer be heard.
Truly, my soul would like to burst out of its shell and beg.
My pain is mute and my crime only wearies me in vain.
No sign of emotion on the hard faces around me.
When I hear their words, I hear only a noise that hurts me,
for nothing replies to me. What fate has befallen me?
Will I have to wander in the desert for all my life?
Is this a dream where I am? Have I ceased to be a man?
The thing that I am now: is it what I always was?

SERVANT

How much longer before they relieve us?

BASSIO

We shan't be relieved. The condemned men will be executed soon
and then we shall escort this man out of Venice.

JAFFIER

Which man is there so low that I might dare, without trembling,
even to raise up my eyes to the level of his knees,
the traitor that I am? However, if I want to live,
then I shall often be forced to find those who with one word
will be able to refuse or to grant me what I need,
always afraid, everywhere, that my treason's been found out.
No matter how fast I walk, rumour will travel faster,
and over all the earth, everywhere that desire goes,
every single look will give me a good cause to tremble.
Where shall I be able to exist and not see humans?
Ah! If only I could exist and never see the sun!
I shall become insane if I am seen by so many.
Leave me, out of pity. I do not want to be insane.

SERVANT

Why don't we just kill him with the others? We don't have to guard him.

BASSIO

This one's not to be killed. He was the one who denounced the others.

JAFFIER

Am I the one who has come to this?
Was I once not loaded with honours,
surrounded by the highest respect?
Have I not been cherished by a friend?
I dreamed. All that was only a dream.
I was always vile. I am vile now.

SERVANT

He's as guilty as the others, and a traitor as well. I don't understand why he's allowed to live.

BASSIO

Their Lordships are too scrupulous when it comes to keeping their word. I for one should be glad to put him to death.

JAFFIER

Death will soon come to put an end to my misery.
Death. And yet, not death. My God, I have no desire to die.
My friend will die; oh, if only I could live forever
so that never, after death, might I be seen by his eyes!
The sun makes me afraid; death, which tears away the last veil,
makes me still more afraid; for death will strip my soul naked.
God, my soul has need of flesh, in order to hide its shame.
Flesh that eats and sleeps, with no future and without a past.
As long as I am alive, I can try to forget this.

The shame that crushes me makes me a wretched man indeed.
I should tremble with horror to pass into eternity;
too feeble for death. But how am I to remain alive?
Those who have lost me ought now to take me into their care.
My distress was all their work, and now I have need of them.
Please tell me, at least, when I shall see your master again.

BASSIO

You will not see him again. You are to leave Venetian territory and are
forbidden ever to return, on pain of death. Once your accomplices
have been executed, we shall take you to the border. Until then, you
do not need to see anybody.

JAFFIER

I must see him again. I want to talk to your master.
Go and request that he has me brought to him once again.

BASSIO

We shall not go. He'd refuse. He has nothing to say to you. You are
banished. Isn't that enough for you?

JAFFIER

Abandoned, I am forced to depart,
overcome with disgrace and distress.
My friends will die, all betrayed by me.
Those whom I have saved by my pity,
having robbed me of honour, ban me.
The brightness of day makes me suffer.
I am weary of my lowered eyes.
If I want to die, I lack the heart.
I do not wish to become insane.

SERVANT

Because of him, we shan't see the festival. I should like to slaughter
him, like a stinking animal.

BASSIO

I think as you do, but don't forget that the Ten have spared his life.

JAFFIER

I leave without friends, banished, deprived of all my honour.
No one wants anything from me, now that I have lost all.
Where can I turn? For who would want to welcome a traitor
when even those whom my treachery saved will banish me?
This can't be happening. I want to talk to your master.
Those who have taken my honour, they know just what I am;
with them alone will I find a refuge against my shame.
Either lead me to your master, or have him brought to me.
Ah! Will you not go and find your master, out of pity?
Must it be, then, that I shall never again see his face,
never hear his voice? And yet I have no one in the world
apart from him, now that my friends have all been put to death.
I am being torn apart. I am being torn apart by pain.
     Alas! My friend, now they torture you.
     And I have been reduced to begging
     these servants and your hangmen in vain.
     Ah! My friend, my friend, how you cry out;
     I hear your screams; why am I not deaf?
     My God, I can neither die nor live.
     My crime was just to have shown pity.

*Enter several artisans and apprentices, who form a group around
Bassio and Jaffier.*

ARTISAN

What's going on, Bassio? What are you doing with all these armed
men?

BASSIO

Ah, you still don't know what's happened? Great things have gone on
while you were asleep. Luckily for you, their Lordships keep vigil.

Venice almost perished this night. Spain had set up a conspiracy and had undermined the loyalty of our troops. Yesterday, Providence made one of these wretches give himself up to the Ten and reveal all. Now the criminals are being interrogated in prison. They will all be put to death.

ARTISAN

Blessed be Heaven for preserving our Venice! Our Venice is as dear to us as she is to the nobles; she belongs to us as much as to them. And that man gazing at the ground – who is he?

BASSIO

He's the one who denounced the others. We're keeping him until all the others are dead, and then we shall banish him from Venetian territory. You men are lucky. You'll see the festival. We can't: because of him.

APPRENTICE

He's not going to be killed? We're going to let one of the dogs live?

BASSIO

Their Lordships have spared his life, because he denounced his accomplices.

APPRENTICE

He is twice a traitor! Allow me to get close to him.
I am curious to see what a traitor looks like, up close.
Raise your head, dog! I want to see the eyes of a coward.
Come on, look at me. Just see how his eyes are free from tears,
though his friends are close, and scream in the hands of the hangman.
We can hear them from here. And death will follow very soon;
in our prison, interrogation does not last for long;
all the secrets that we need are yielded very quickly.
This wretch you have is more despicable than the others.
Look at him. Do we really have to let such a man live?

Just seeing him disgusts me. I should be pleased to strangle him.

BASSIO

Don't touch him. Traitor, get behind me. He is under my protection.

APPRENTICE

No, do not hide him. I want to look at him one last time.
Move aside a little; let me see him; I beg of you.
Is it really possible that such vile things could exist?
Why does he refuse to speak? I should like to hear his voice.
Let me strike him, so that we can at least hear him cry out.
Look at how he trembles! Look at how he bows down his head.
A traitor is always a coward. Please may I strike him?
No, you do not want me to? While his accomplices die,
the man who betrayed them is allowed to be without pain?
Traitor! Traitor! Do you hear? Look, the word makes him tremble.
Do you realize how vile that man is, who has sold his friends?
That a traitor preserved our Venice is an affliction.
You say that the Ten have been forced to promise him his life,
but if I killed him without their order, they would be glad,
for perhaps his life could be a danger to our city.
If I were the one to kill him, who did not take an oath,
I should not wound my honour, nor the honour of the Ten,
and our act would have been in the interest of our city.
Can we really contemplate keeping this coward alive?
Come on! What do you say? Give me permission to kill him!

BASSIO

I only wish I could give you permission; I think as you do. He disgusts me. He has deserved a thousand deaths, and I fear that later he will harm Venice. A traitor is always ungrateful; he will not thank Venice for the life he has been granted. What is more: he is capable of any crime, of any act of cowardice. And then, if he were dead, I'd be able to go and enjoy the festival. It's horrible for me, to have to spend the day of the festival guarding vermin like this. But what do you want? I cannot allow him to be killed on Venetian territory. My

master ordered me to take him away from Venetian territory; I shall
do so. I hope he will not live long afterwards.

APPRENTICE

Doubtless he will not live long. Whom would he not horrify?
For even the criminals would refuse to take him in.
The earth would be horrified to carry him for longer.
And, dear companions, the Heaven that protects Venice
is eager to be seen to destroy all her enemies.
What great joy today for us all, the people of Venice,
this queen of the seas where the most humble man is a king,
to see our city, on the day of its loveliest feast,
delivered by miracle from the peril that threatened!

BASSIO

Ah! That was the signal announcing that all the conspirators have
been put to death.

ARTISAN

All the better. *They* can't do any more harm to Venice. Let's forget
them; let's just think of our happiness and the festival.

APPRENTICE

Your friends are all of them dead, the friends whom you have sold.
All dead. Do you hear? He says nothing. He has understood.
I think he is going to speak. The traitor speaks! Listen.

JAFFIER

At last, it is finished. [25] And now I should like to sleep.

BASSIO

What you are going to do now is to leave. And quickly. Move
yourself! You have to go.

JAFFIER

Go where? I have nowhere I can go.

BASSIO

Anywhere you want. Away from Venice. And fast. Come with me
and take the gold their Lordships have granted you. The wages of
treason. Come on! Take the gold.

JAFFIER

Thank you. I shall be able to hide, to sleep and to eat.

APPRENTICE

No, not another step! See, thanks to his two betrayals
he leaves, laden with gold, rich and happy and gorged on crimes!
Do not hold me back; this man is as vile as Judas was;
I want to spit on him. Coward, you won't go much further.
Traitor, traitor, this gold is the blood of all of your friends!
He's afraid. Can you see? All his body trembles with fear.
Grant me permission to go with you up to the border;
and then I'll kill him, away from Venice, at my leisure.
Will you not consent? It is too unjust for him to live.

ARTISAN

Shut up for a moment. All of you. What's this noise from the nearby
streets? Can you hear it?

BASSIO

One of you go and see what it is.

Exit servant.

ARTISAN

It sounds like a fight. I hear screams. It's still not finished; something
is going on. Could Venice be still in danger?

BASSIO

May Heaven confound her enemies!

APPRENTICE

We shall defend her if we must.

ARTISAN

But Heaven forbid that we have to fight to save her on this day of the festival!

BASSIO

We'll go see what it is.

APPRENTICE

He looks pleased.

Servant returns.

BASSIO

What is it? Speak fast!

SERVANT

It's very little. A handful of these bandits were able to escape from the wise measures taken this night by their Lordships. They're all there now, armed, trying to defend themselves. But half of them have been slaughtered already, and soon they'll all be dead; forces still loyal to Venice are there in number, and are cutting them to pieces easily enough. Soon they'll all be done for. The battle is taking place near here, in the streets.

BASSIO

Heaven be praised! I feared the worst.

ARTISAN

We shall have a peaceful day, in spite of everything.

BASSIO

Who'd have thought we could have a peaceful day with enemies like this in our midst? But some of them have been executed in prison; the others will be killed in a few moments. That will be a lesson, I hope, for anyone thinking of attacking Venice. It will be a long time, I reckon, before anybody tries it again.

APPRENTICE

That sort of death is too good for people like that. They shouldn't find death in combat. They ought to die at the hand of the hangman.

BASSIO

It doesn't matter how they die, as long as our Venice is rid of these vermin! They can't harm her any longer. May all her enemies end this way!

ARTISAN

But look at the traitor; we forgot about him. What's going on? He's dropped his gold; he dares to raise his head and look around.

SERVANT

He might be off to join the fight. Should we stop him?

BASSIO

Absolutely not! Let him go. Just follow him. If he goes and joins these bandits, he'll be slaughtered with them, and we'll be rid of him, and Venice will not have broken her word. We couldn't wish for anything better. Just let him go!

ARTISAN

He's stopped. See how he smiles. Has he gone insane?

BASSIO

The chance is too good to miss. If he doesn't go, we'll force him. He needs to go and get himself killed.

ARTISAN

He seems to be going.

BASSIO

Then let him get a move on, so that all this can be over! I can see my master's daughter over there. She could be coming here. She knows nothing. She must not learn of anything. These dangers and all the blood that has been spilled: it could spoil the festival for her. Three of you are to follow the traitor; let him pick up a sword, if he wants to die with a sword in his hand; what does that matter to us? But push him out there if he hesitates for too long, so that he can be massacred with the others as soon as possible. The rest of you, sheathe your swords, move off and not a word about what has happened.

ARTISAN

He's stopped moving again.

SERVANT

What should we do?

BASSIO

Let's wait a little. Let's see what he's going to do.

JAFFIER

Death is going to come for me. For now, the shame has passed.
To eyes that will soon go dark, how lovely is the city!

I must leave the land of the living, never to return.
There will be no dawn where I shall go, nor any city.

BASSIO

My master's daughter is here. Quickly, let's go. Let's push him into death.

Exeunt.

VIOLETTA

Loveliest day, now suddenly you're there,
on my city and its thousand canals;
those humans who now receive your smile
      see how sweet you are!

Never before have I slept, till last night!
My heart could drink and drink till sleep was dry.
Then the sweet day came, to my eyes
      lovelier than sleep!

The day so long awaited is now here,
touching the city of stone and water.
All around me is a gentle shiver
      in the still air.

Your bliss is there; come and see, my city.
Spouse of the sea, look far and look near.
So many high tides, such happy murmurs
      bless your awakening!

Daylight comes across the sea slowly.
Soon the feast will fulfil every desire.
The calm sea waits. How lovely on this sea
      are the rays of day!

Curtain

Notes

Chapter 3

1 The idea of self-annihilation was certainly not new in the mystical tradition. An important precedent can be found in Meister Eckhart (see Robert 2012).

Simone Weil's Notes on *Venice Saved*

1 The numbers in square brackets indicate an endnote by the editors.

Further Reading

1 The texts *Attente de Dieu* and *Lettre à un Religieux*, known in English as *Waiting on God/Waiting for God* and *Letter to a Priest* respectively, were retranslated in one volume in 2012 as *Awaiting God*, with an introduction by Sylvie Weil, who notes how the link between paying attention and compassion is at the heart of *Venice Saved* (2012: 15.)

2 See endnote 1.

Translators' Notes

[1]
The remarks preceding the play are taken from Simone Weil's notebooks and were included in the 1968 edition, the source text for this translation.

[2]
The 'social' is a key term for Weil and is discussed in Chapter 2.

[3]
The expression 'Having roots' translates the French 'L'enracinement', which is the title of the book by Weil translated as *The Need for Roots* (2002a). Imagery of rootedness is found in both the paratext and the text of *Venice Saved*. Again, see Chapter 2.

[4]
The noun 'affliction' translates the French *malheur*, a key term in Weil: see Chapter 3 for a discussion of the term and Chapter 4 for the translation issue.

[5]
Job, a righteous man from the Land of Uz, is afflicted by a series of terrible troubles, such as the loss of his wealth, his children and his servants. Covered in boils, he sits on a dung heap and pleads his cause before God, who shows him the wonders of creation. At the end of the story, his prosperity is restored. The Book of Job was one of the Old Testament texts that Weil accepted: see Note [13].

[6]
The Greek *metaxu* signifies 'between' or 'middle ground'. In Plato's *Symposium*, Socrates recounts how the priestess Diotima defines Eros the God of Love as occupying the middle ground between mortality and immortality (202e). It is a common theme in the *Notebooks* and some remarks on the notion are included in *Gravity and Grace*, where Weil describes this world as a closed door that is at once a barrier and a way through, employing the image of two

prisoners in neighbouring cells, who communicate by knocking on the wall, so that the thing that separates them also allows them to communicate: 'Every separation is a link' (GG 145). Gabriela Fiori argues that Weil wanted to be 'a bridge, a route, a *metaxu* of mercy, the only real action' (1989: 251). For J.P. Little, the city of Venice itself is a *metaxu* on account of its independence: it is a 'way of mediation for its citizens' (1979: 302).

[7]
The third dimension: that of transcendence, an image taken from Euclidean geometry.

Oedipus Rex and *The Bacchae* are Greek tragedies by Sophocles and Euripides respectively. Perhaps Weil is indicating that the characters in these plays attain insight through attention.

[8]
Weil's mother wrote to her about Spirituals in July 1943, expressing the hope that she would be able to bring Simone the gift of a recording by Marian Anderson. Weil attended services in black churches in Harlem while in New York. Weil herself wrote to Charles Bell that suffering people often express themselves through 'anonymous melodies, songs, legends, religions' in ways that surpass the greatest geniuses (SL 104).

[9]
Paul Valéry (1871–45) was a French poet to whom Weil sent her poetry for comment. (See Chapter 4.) An heir of Stéphane Mallarmé, he wrote sparse poetry in traditional verse forms that play 'on the threshold of the physical and the metaphysical' and that create opportunities for 'patient meditation', according to John Lyons (2010: 94).

[10]
The Abbé de Saint-Réal (1643–92) published his historical fiction in 1674, as discussed in Chapters 1 and 2.

[11]
Doge Pietro II Orseolo of Venice conquered Dalmatia in 1000 and instituted a commemoration of the victory, to take place every

Ascension Day. John Julius Norwich writes, 'Later, as the tradition grew more venerable, so the ceremony grew more elaborate, and included the casting of a propitiatory golden ring into the waves; thus it was slowly to become identified with a symbolic marriage to the sea – the *Sposalizio del Mar* – a character that it was to retain until the end of the Republic itself' (2003: 55). The ceremony still takes place in Venice. Weil sets it at Pentecost, which is when the conspirators were to take over Venice.

[12]

The play makes an oblique but fierce criticism of colonialism. Weil opposed both French colonialism and the role played by the Catholic Church in colonial expansion. In contrast to many contemporary theologians, however, there is no sustained analysis in Weil's work of the imperialistic aspect of Christianity.

[13]

As noted in Chapter 1, Weil generally disliked and rejected the Old Testament because it portrayed a violent God, so that to 'evoke the Old Testament' means evoking the brutal God of Battles. She did, however, find some of its books amenable to the Christian spirit, that is, 'Isaiah, Job, the Song of Solomon, Tobias, part of Ezekiel, part of the Psalms, part of the Books of Wisdom, the beginning of Genesis' (LP 41). Weil's attitude to the God of the Old Testament is found in Christian Gnostic writings generally, in the teachings of Marcion (c.85–c.160) and in Cathar belief (see SL 129–31), all of which are heretical by Catholic standards.

[14]

According to the *samkhya* and *yoga* systems of Indian philosophy, the Sanskrit term *guna* represents the three qualities of the universe: *sattva* (truth), *tamas* (darkness) and *rajas* (passion). *Rajas* is a passion that is typically associated with warriors, hence its relevance here. The *gunas* are prominent in *The Bhagavad Gita*, a book that Weil read in French in 1940 and in Sanskrit in 1941 and that was very important to her for its depiction of Arjuna, a reluctant warrior who engages in a disputation with Krishna, who at last convinces him to make war against his cousins, providing that he acts with detachment. (See Chapter 3.) Laurie L. Patton gives a full explanation of the *gunas* in the introduction to her translation of the *Gita* (2008: xviii–xix). Weil discusses *rajas* in the *Notebooks*, calling it 'of the nature of passion, giving rise to thirst and attachment', and stating that its fruit is pain (NB 92).

[15]

Weil frequently describes morality in terms taken from the physical sciences, as in the following quotation: 'All the natural movements of the soul are controlled by laws analogous to those of physical gravity. Grace is the only exception' (GG: 1). Such metaphors are typical of Platonic philosophy and can be found, for example, in Plotinus and Augustine.

[16]

Claudio Monteverdi (1567–1643) was one of the greatest Italian composers. He came to Venice in 1613 to direct the music at Saint Mark's Basilica and remained there until his death, so he would have been active in Venice at the time of the conspiracy.

[17]

Carthage was destroyed by the Romans in 146 BCE under the generalship of Scipio Africanus, who is said to have wept as the city burned, foreseeing the destruction of Rome in its turn, according to Polybius. Weil describes how the beauty of Bourges fell before the force of Caesar's Roman army, the Gauls being unable to destroy it of their own accord (NR 219) and also refers to how the Carthaginians offered their own lives in order to save their city (2002a: 169). Little remarks that it is 'the fragility of these cities [Bourges, Carthage, Venice, Troy, the Cathar strongholds of the Languedoc] in the face of military might which captures Simone Weil's imagination' (1979: 303). (See also Note [20].)

[18]

Hernán Cortés (1485–1547) was the Spanish Conquistador responsible for the downfall of the Aztec Empire and the beginning of the Spanish colonization of the Americas.

[19]

These words are in English in Weil's text, taken from Christopher Marlowe's *Tamburlaine the Great* Act Two Scene Seven (1973). The play was written in 1577 or 1578 and shows Tamburlaine's inexorable military ascent from Scythian shepherd to emperor. He thus swears never to rest:

> Until we reach the ripest bliss of all,
> That perfect bliss and sole felicity,
> The sweet fruition of an earthly crown.

The image is used in French in Renaud's long speech later in this act.

[20]

Carthage, Cartagena and Persepolis are examples of conquered cities. Carthage was destroyed by the Romans in 146 BCE: see Note [17]. Cartegena or New Carthage was a Carthaginian colony in Spain that fell to Rome in 210 BCE. The Persian city Persepolis was destroyed by Alexander the Great in 330 BCE. Venice is thus again seen as an archetype of the beauty of the world, threatened by military might.

[21]

Plutarch (c.46–120) was a Greek historian known for his *Parallel Lives*, biographies of famous Greeks and Romans that are studies in worldly greatness.

[22]

Cardinal de Retz (1613–79) wrote a celebrated autobiography, the *Mémoires*, which Weil liked, telling Pétrement that she admired 'not only the profundity of his views on the political struggles but also his character, the feelings of a man who above all esteemed will, resolution, and lucidity' (Pétrement 1976: 142). Retz also wrote an essay about the conspiracy of Giovanni Luigi Fieschi (usually known as Fiesco) in Genoa in 1547. Andrée Mansau comments that Saint-Réal shares with Retz the 'glory of uniting history, morality, politics and psychology', but that in addition he is a 'creator 'who introduces themes of 'madness, love and death' (1977: 4; our translation).

[23]

Niobe, wife of Amphion, King of Thebes, had six sons and six daughters. When she boasted that she had more children than Leto, mother of Apollo and Artemis, Apollo killed Niobe's sons and Artemis her daughters to avenge the insult. Weil translates the passage in *Iliad 24* about this legend in her essay on Homer (1999). The courtesan's desire for revenge goes beyond justice to a vengefulness that is reminiscent of the Old Testament ethic that Weil could not accept.

[24]

Plautus (c.254–184 BCE) was a writer of Latin comedies. His plays feature slaves in prominent roles, typically as trickster figures, who are liable to a wide variety of horrific punishments (which they usually manage to avoid, given that these are comedies). They often speak at length about torture. Weil writes, 'There appears in Plautus one characteristic of a slave; e.g., an obsession with punishments' (LPW 101). The reference here thus seems to be generic.

[25]

The final utterance of the crucified Jesus of Nazareth is given in Hellenistic Greek by John (19.30) as 'Tetelestai' (it has been finished), which is translated by the King James Bible as 'It is finished'.

Bibliography

Bakewell, S. (2016), *At the Existentialist Café*, London: Chatto and Windus.

de Balzac, H. [1835] (1966), *Le Père Goriot*, Paris: Garnier-Flammarion.

Bellos, D. (2018), 'Easy Peasy', *In Other Words*, Vol. 50: 60–6.

Benjamin, W. [1923] (2012), 'The Translator's Task', tr. by S. Rendall, in L. Venuti (ed.), *The Translation Studies Reader* [Third Edition], London and New York: Routledge, 75–83.

The Bhagavad Gita (2008), tr. by L. L. Patton, London: Penguin.

Boase-Beier, J. (2015), *Translating the Poetry of the Holocaust*, London: Bloomsbury.

Boase-Beier, J., and M. Holman (eds) (1999), *The Practices of Literary Translation*, Manchester: St. Jerome.

Brueck, T. (1995), *The Redemption of Tragedy: The Literary Vision of Simone Weil*, New York: SUNY Press.

Cabaud Meaney, M. (2007), *Simone Weil's Apologetic Use of Literature: Her Christological Interpretations of Ancient Greek Texts*, Oxford and New York: Oxford University Press.

Campo, C. (tr.) (1987), *Simone Weil: Venezia Salva*, Milan: Adelphi.

Carson, Anne (2005), *Decreation: Poetry, Essays, Opera*, London: Jonathan Cape.

Clack, B. (2015), 'Feminist Approaches to Religion', in G. Oppy (ed.), *The Routledge Handbook of Contemporary Philosophy of Religion*, London and New York: Routledge, 7–19.

Constantine, D. (2004), *A Living Language*, Newcastle: Bloodaxe.

Critchley, S. (2001), *Continental Philosophy*, Oxford: Oxford University Press.

Drury, J. (2014), *Music at Midnight: The Life and Poetry of George Herbert*, London: Penguin.

Eagleton, T. (2007), *How to Read a Poem*, Oxford: Blackwell.

An Encounter with Simone Weil (2011) [Film], Dir. J. Haslett, USA: Passion River Films.

Fiori, G. (1989), *Simone Weil: An Intellectual Biography*, tr. by J. R. Berrigan, Athens and London: University of Georgia Press.

Gaeta, F. (1970), 'Giorgio da Trebisonda, le "Leggi" di Platone e la costituzione di Venezia', *Bullettino dell'Istituto storico per il Medioevo*, Vol. LXXXII: 479–501.

Gaeta, G. (n.d.), 'Venezia salva: L'ideale politico di una città a misura d'uomo', available online: http://www.veneziasalva.it/1/chi_siamo_5 20104.html (accessed 15 May 2018).

Gross, P. (2018), 'Mind the Gap', *The Author*, Vol. CXXIX, No.1: 11–12.

Hadot, P. (1995), *Philosophy as a Way of Life*, tr. by M. Chase, Oxford: Blackwell.

Hamburger, M. (tr.) (2007), *Friedrich Hölderlin: Selected Poems and Fragments*, London: Penguin.

Hazareesingh, S. (2015), *How the French Think*, London: Allen Lane.

Hillgarth, J. N. (2000), *The Mirror of Spain, 1500–1700: The Formation of a Myth*, Ann Arbor: University of Michigan Press.

von Hofmannsthal, H. (1905), *Das gerettete Venedig*, Berlin: Fischer.

Hutchison, K., and F. Jenkins (eds) (2013), *Women in Philosophy*, Oxford: Oxford University Press.

Jakobson, R. [1959] (2012), 'On Linguistic Aspects of Translation', in L. Venuti (ed.), *The Translation Studies Reader* [Third Edition], London and New York: Routledge, 126–31.

Large, D. (2019), 'The Translation of Philosophical Texts', in P. Rawling and P. Wilson (eds), *The Routledge Handbook of Translation and Philosophy*, London and New York: Routledge.

Little, J. P. (1979), 'Society as Mediator in Simone Weil's "Venise Sauvée"', *Modern Languages Review*, Vol. 65, No. 2: 289–305.

de Lussy, F. (1999a), 'Vie et œuvre', in S. Weil (ed.), *Œuvres*, Paris: Gallimard, 35–93.

Lyons, J.D. (2010), *French Literature: A Very Short Introduction*, Oxford: Oxford University Press.

Mansau, A. (1977), 'Introduction', in Saint-Réal, M. l'abbé de [César Vichard] [1674] (1977), *Don Carlos; La conjuration des Espagnols contre la république de Venise*, Geneva: Droz, 1–47.

Marlowe, C. (1999), *Tamburlaine the Great*, Manchester: Manchester University Press.

McCullough, L. (2014), *The Religious Philosophy of Simone Weil*, London and New York: I.B. Tauris.

Miles, S. (ed.) (2005), *Simone Weil: An Anthology*, London: Penguin.

Nevin, T. (2000), *Simone Weil: Portrait of a Self-exiled Jew*, Chapel Hill: University of North Carolina Press.

Nono, S. (n.d.), 'Director's Notes', available online: http://www.veneziasalva.it/2/ (accessed 18 May 2018).

Norwich, J. J. (2003), *A History of Venice*, London: Penguin.

O'Brien, R. (2018), 'Can verse drama survive?' *The Author*, Vol. CXXIX, No. 1: 23–4.

Otway, T. [1682] (1976), *Venice Preserv'd*, in R. G. Lawrence (ed.), *Restoration Plays*, London: Everyman, 237–309.

Pétrement, S. (1976), *Simone Weil: A Life*, tr. by R. Rosenthal, London and Oxford: Mowbrays.

Plant, S. (2007), *The SPCK Introduction to Simone Weil*, London: SPCK.

Plato [c. 380 BCE] (1994), *Symposium*, tr. by R. Waterfield, Oxford: Oxford University Press.

Plato [c. 380 BCE] (1998), *The Republic*, tr. by R. Waterfield, Oxford: Oxford University Press.

Preto, P. (1996), 'La 'congiura di Bedmar' a Venezia nel 1618: colpo di Stato o provocazione?' *Actes du colloque international organisé à Rome, 30 septembre - 2 octobre 1993*, Publications de l'École Française de Rome, 289–315.

Rawling, P., and P. Wilson (eds) (2019), *The Routledge Handbook of Translation and Philosophy*, London and New York: Routledge.

Rée, J. (2001), 'The Translation of Philosophy', *New Literary History*, Vol. 32, No. 2: 223–57.

Rees, R. (1958), *Brave Men: A Study of D.H. Lawrence and Simone Weil*, Carbondale: Southern Illinois University Press.

Robert, W. (2012), 'A Mystic Impulse: From Apophatics to Decreation in Pseudo-Dionysius, Meister Eckhart, and Simone Weil' *Medieval Mystical Theology*, Vol 21, No. 1: 113–32.

Saarhario, K. (2013) [Musical oratorio], *La Passion de Simone*, libretto by A. Maalouf, Finland: Ondine.

Saint-Réal, M. l'abbé de [César Vichard] [1674] (1977), *Don Carlos; La conjuration des Espagnols contre la république de Venise*, Geneva: Droz.

Sarpi, P. (1834), 'Congiura ordita da Piero Giron di Ossuna vicerè di Napoli, 3 dicembre 1618,' in Aurelio Bianchi-Giovini (ed.), *Storia di Venezia*, Mendrisio: Capolago.

Scholem, G. (1996), *On the Kabbalah and its Symbolism*, tr. by R. Manheim, New York: Schocken.

Sontag, S. (1963), '*Simone Weil: Selected Essays*, translated by Richard Rees', *New York Review of Books*, February 1.

Taleb, N. N. (2018), *Skin in the Game*, London: Allen Lane.

Tamás, R. (2017), *Savage*, London: Clinic Press.

Venezia Salva (2013) [Film], Dir. S. Nono, Italy: Giano con Rai Cinema.

Vetö, M. (1994), *The Religious Metaphysics of Simone Weil*, tr. by J. Dargan, Albany, NY: SUNY Press.

Weil, S. [1951] (1956), *The Notebooks of Simone Weil*, tr. by A. Wills, London and New York: Routledge. [2 volumes].

Weil, S. (1957), *Intimations of Christianity among the Ancient Greeks*, tr. by E. Chase Geissbuhler, London and New York: Routledge.

Weil, S. (1965), *Seventy Letters*, tr. by R. Rees, London: Oxford University Press.

Weil, S. [1955] (1968), *Poèmes suivis de Venise sauvée, Lettre de Paul Valéry*, Paris: Gallimard.

Weil, S. [1950] (1978), *Waiting on God*, tr. by E. Craufurd, Glasgow: Collins/Fontana.

Weil, S. (1999), *Œuvres*, Paris: Gallimard.

Weil, S. [1955] (2001), *Oppression and Liberty*, tr. by A. Wills and J. Petrie, London and New York: Routledge.

Weil, S. [1949] (2002a), *The Need for Roots*, tr. by A. Wills, London and New York: Routledge.

Weil, S. [1951] (2002b), *Letter to a Priest*, tr. by A. Wills, London and New York: Routledge.

Weil, S. [1947] (2003), *Gravity and Grace*, tr. by E. Craufurd and M. von der Ruhr, London and New York: Routledge.

Weil, S. [1940] (2005), 'The Iliad, or The Poem of Force', in S. Weil and R. Bespaloff (eds), *War and the Iliad*, tr. by M. McCarthy, New York: New York Review Books, 3–37.

Weil, S. [Sylvie] (2009), *Chez les Weil*, Paris: Libretto.

Weil, S. [1950/1951] (2012), *Awaiting God*, tr. by B. Jersak, Abbotsford: Fresh Wind Press.

Weil, S. [1940] (2014), *On the Abolition of All Political Parties*, tr. by S. Leys, New York: NYRB Classics.

Weil, S. (2015), *Late Philosophical Writings*, tr. by E. O. Springsted and L. E. Schmidt, Notre Dame, Indiana: University of Notre Dame Press.

Weinberger, E., and O. Paz (1987), *19 Ways of Looking at Wang Wei*, London: Asphodel.

Wilson, P. (2016), *Translation after Wittgenstein*, London and New York: Routledge.

Wittgenstein, L. (1973), *Letters to C.K. Ogden*, Oxford: Blackwell.

Wittgenstein, L. [1953] (2009), *Philosophical Investigations*, tr. by G. E. M. Anscombe, P. M. S. Hacker and J. Schulte, Chichester: Wiley-Blackwell.

Further Reading

Websites

www.americanweilsociety.org

(The website of the American Weil Society. The site as a whole is recommended. It contains a very detailed bibliography.)

www.simoneweil-association.com

(The French website of the Association pour l'Étude de la Pensée de Simone Weil (Association for the Study of the Thought of Simone Weil). There is a link to the *Cahiers Simone Weil* (Notebooks Simone Weil), a French review of Weil's thought that includes one article in English in each edition.)

Chapter 1

An Encounter with Simone Weil (2011), (Film) Dir. J. Haslett, USA: Passion River Films. (Julia Haslett's film is an interesting personal take on Weil's relevance for the twenty-first century, looking at her demand that we pay attention to a suffering world.)

Fiori, G. (1989), *Simone Weil: An Intellectual Biography*, tr. by J. R. Berrigan, Athens and London: University of Georgia Press. (The book traces the development of Weil's thought in relation to the major events of the times. Contains many suggestions for further reading.)

Miles, S. (ed.) (2005), *Simone Weil: An Anthology*, London: Penguin. (A collection of texts that forms a good place to start for those with no knowledge of Weil's work.)

Pétrement, S. (1976), *Simone Weil: A Life*, tr. by R. Rosenthal, London and Oxford: Mowbrays. (The first biography of Weil. It is very readable and particularly interesting because it is the work of Weil's lifelong friend.)

Plant, S. (2007), *The SPCK Introduction to Simone Weil*, London: SPCK. (A short and insightful presentation of her life and thought. Contains excellent suggestions for further reading.)

Weil, S. [1951] (1956) *The Notebooks of Simone Weil*, tr. by A. Wills, London and New York: Routledge. [2 volumes] (Weil's *Cahiers*, which form the source for *Gravity and Grace*, show her unedited thoughts

across a range of subjects and make fascinating reading. This edition
of her notebooks concludes with her story in which she encounters
a mysterious figure who leads her to a church, even though she has
not been baptized, and she reflects: 'And yet deep down within me
something, a particle of myself, cannot help thinking, with fear and
trembling, that perhaps, in spite of all, he loves me' [NB 639].)

Weil, S. (1965) *Seventy Letters*, tr. by R. Rees, London: Oxford
University Press. (Many authors are at their most accessible in their
correspondence and Weil is no exception. This selection from her many
letters effectively forms an autobiography.)

Weil, S. (2001) *Oppression and Liberty*, tr. by A. Wills and J. Petrie,
London: Routledge. (The earlier political thought.)

Weil, S. [1949] (2002a) *The Need for Roots*, tr. by A. Wills, London and
New York: Routledge. (The later political thought.)

Weil, S. [1951] (2002b) *Letter to a Priest*, tr. by A. Wills, London and
New York: Routledge. (A collection of pieces that represents an
overview of Weil's mystical take on religion in the context of her desire
for baptism and simultaneous recognition that it is impossible for her.)[1]

Chapter 2

Little, J. P. (1979), 'Society as Mediator in Simone Weil's "Venise
Sauvée"', *Modern Languages Review*, Vol. 65, No. 2: 289–305.
(An essay explaining the political significance of *Venice Saved* and its
links with Weil's ideas in *The Need for Roots*.)

Mackenney, R. (2000), '"A Plot Discover'd"?: Myth, Legend and the
"Spanish" Conspiracy against Venice in 1618', in J. Martin and
D. Romano (eds), *Venice Reconsidered: The History and Civilisation of
an Italian City-State, 1297–1797*, Baltimore: John Hopkins University
Press. (A historical exploration of the truth and the myth in the Spanish
conspiracy on which *Venice Saved* is based.)

Otway, T. [1682] (1976), *Venice Preserv'd*, in R. G. Lawrence (ed.),
Restoration Plays, London: Everyman, 237–309. (For a quite different
take on the same source used by Weil.)

Saint-Réal, M. l'abbé de [César Vichard] [1674] (1977), *Don Carlos; La
conjuration des Espagnols contre la république de Venise*, Geneva:
Droz. (The second account here is Weil's main source for her play.)

Weil, S. [1949] (2002), *The Need for Roots*, tr. by A. Wills, London
and New York: Routledge. (Where Weil describes many of the ideas

that are found in the play, especially the meaning and importance of
'rootedness' for the human soul.)

Weil, S. (2014), *On the Abolition of All Political Parties*, tr. by Simon
Leys, New York: New York Review. (Includes Weil's thoughts on the
dangers of the 'collective' with a clear and helpful preface by Czesław
Miłosz.)

Chapter 3

Brueck, Katherine T. (1995), *The Redemption of Tragedy: The Literary
Vision of Simone Weil*, New York: SUNY Press. (An analysis of Weil's
thoughts on literary works, based on Weil's philosophy, but from
the perspective of literary studies; it presents Weil's supernaturalist
perspective as an alternative to post-structuralist literary theory.)

Cabaud Meaney, M. (2007), *Simone Weil's Apologetic Use of Literature:
Her Christological Interpretations of Ancient Greek Texts*, Oxford and
New York: Oxford University Press. (A perceptive reading of Weil's
original Christian interpretation of Greek texts, especially Chapter 4 on
Antigone.)

Weil, S. (1957), *Intimations of Christianity among the Ancient Greeks*, tr.
by E. Chase Geissbuhler, London: Routledge. (The collection of Weil's
writings on classical ancient texts, from Plato to the Greek tragedians.)

Weil, S. [1950] (1978), *Waiting on God*, tr. by E. Craufurd, Glasgow:
Collins/Fontana. (Containing Weil's reflections on beauty, friendship
and her letters to Joseph-Marie Perrin on spiritual matters.)[2]

Vetö, M. (1994), *The Religious Metaphysics of Simone Weil*, tr. by
J. Dargan, Albany, NY: SUNY Press. (An excellent study of Weil's
metaphysics, including key concepts such as decreation, affliction and
attention.)

Chapter 4

Barnstone, W. (1993), *The Poetics of Translation*, New Haven and London:
Yale University Press. (A discussion of literary translation by a poet
and translator of poetry. Barnstone stresses that the standards of routine
information transfer do not apply to the translation of literature and
relates translation to the quest for transcendence: 'A translation is a
FRIENDSHIP between poets. There is a mystical union between them
based on love and art' [1993: 268].)

Bellos, D. (2011), *Is That a Fish in Your Ear?* London: Particular Books. (A fascinating and accessible introduction to the issues that arise when translating from one language into another.)

Benjamin, W. [1923] (2012), 'The Translator's Task', tr. by S. Rendall, in L. Venuti (ed.), *The Translation Studies Reader* [Third edition], London and New York: Routledge, 75–83. (A difficult but enormously influential statement on translation. As the title suggests, it is more about how the translator should see his or her task than about how to translate, a point often not noted by critics.)

Rawling, P., and P. Wilson (2019), *The Routledge Handbook of Translation and Philosophy*, London and New York: Routledge. (Surveys the links between translation and philosophy in four parts: philosophers on translation; translation studies and philosophy; the translation of philosophy; and emerging trends.)

Weil, S. [1940] (1999), 'L'Iliade ou le poème de la force', in F. de Lussy (ed.), *Œuvres*, Paris: Gallimard, 527–52. (Weil's translations of Homer are found here; for an English translation, see IP.)

Weinberger, E., and O. Paz (1987), *19 Ways of Looking at Wang Wei*, London: Asphodel. (A short but fascinating book that shows how one four-line lyric by the Chinese poet Wang Wei can be and has been translated in many ways, to different effects. The best translations, it is argued, result from a complete humility before the text.)

Index